The Mixtecans
of Juxtlahuaca,
Mexico

The Mixtecans
of Juxtlahuaca,
Mexico

Kimball Romney
Romaine Romney

 ROBERT E. KRIEGER PUBLISHING COMPANY
HUNTINGTON, NEW YORK

Original Edition 1966
Reprint 1973

Printed and Published by
ROBERT E. KRIEGER PUBLISHING CO., INC.
BOX 542, HUNTINGTON, NEW YORK, 11743

©Copyright by
John Wiley & Sons, Inc.
Reprinted by Arrangement

Library of Congress Catalog Card Number: 66-17616
ISBN 0-88275-136-0

Printed in U.S.A. by
NOBLE OFFSET PRINTERS, INC.
New York, N.Y. 10003

Introduction

The six monographs in this series report research undertaken in 1954 by a group of social scientists from Harvard, Yale, and Cornell universities. In its broadest conception, the research aimed at exploring cross-culturally the relation between different patterns of child rearing and subsequent differences in personality. The overall research was designed to study the degree to which the experiences of a child in the first years of life determine his behavior and in adult life influence his perception of the world, his philosophy, religion, and code of ethics.

Theories of the relationship between specific types of treatment in early childhood and subsequent personality differences have been advanced by psychologists and anthropologists. This project was established with the hope of being able to test some of these hypotheses using material collected in a standard manner in six parts of the world where families have divergent ways of life and theories and methods of training young children.

The intellectual history of this project begins with the work of Margaret Mead, Ruth Benedict, Edward Sapir, Ralph Linton, Abram Kardiner, John Dollard, and other pioneers in the field of culture and personality whose work formed the foundation of this study. To detail the contribution of these pioneers would demand an essay on the entire new discipline that grew out of the integration of anthropological and psychological theory, an undertaking not practical in this introduction. A brief historical summary by John Whiting appears in the preface to Volume I of this series.

Specifically, the impetus for the present study came from the cross-cultural work on socialization done by two of the senior investigators, John W. M. Whiting and Irvin L. Child, while they were colleagues at the Institute of Human Relations at Yale University. The results of this research were published in *Child Training and Personality* (1953). Using theories of disease as measures of adult personality, the authors attempted to test certain psychological theories relating the treatment of the basic behavior systems in infancy and childhood to adult personality characteristics.

The data on the 75 societies used in these studies were taken from published ethnographies which varied greatly in detail and areas of coverage. The dream of the investigators was to send field teams out to get comparable detailed material on 100 societies. As a first step in accomplishing this aim, the present study was planned.

In 1953 the Committee on Social Behavior of the Social Science Research Council sponsored a seminar* and a conference† to discuss cross-cultural work on socialization. As a result, the *Field Manual for the Cross-Cultural Study of Child Rearing* was prepared (Whiting et al., 1953), and Whiting and Child persuaded William W. Lambert of Cornell University to join them in seeking funds to conduct a comparative study of child rearing. A generous grant from the Behavioral Science Division of the Ford Foundation made it possible to carry out these plans. The fieldwork and part of the analysis and writing of five of the six reports in this volume were financed by this grant. Later analysis and editing were supported by a grant from the United States Public Health Service.

Intensive planning for the study was carried on at Cornell, Harvard, and Yale during the following year under the direction of the senior investigators, William W. Lambert, Irvin L. Child, and John W. M. Whiting. As part of the over-all research plan, further cross-cultural studies were undertaken at Cornell, Harvard, and Yale. Irvin Child, with the assistance of Margaret Bacon and Herbert Barry, investigated the consequences of various types of training on nurturance, responsibility, obedience, self-reliance, and achievement using ethnographic accounts for cross-cultural comparison (Bacon, Child, and Barry, 1963; Barry, Bacon, and Child, 1957; Barry, Child, and Bacon, 1959). William Lambert and Leigh Minturn did further cross-cultural work on aggres-

---

* The contributing members of the seminar were Barbara Chartier Ayers, Hildreth Geertz, George Goethals, Charles Holzinger, Edgar Lowell, Eleanor E. Maccoby, A. Kimball Romney, Richard Salisbury, William Steward, and John W. Thibaut.

† Attending the conference were Robert R. Sears (Chairman), A. L. Baldwin, R. A. Bauer, Irvin L. Child, L. S. Cottrell, Jr., Leon Festinger, J. G. Gewirtz, A. Inkeles, Harry Levin, Gardner Lindzey, Eleanor E. Maccoby, Carson McGuire, G. P. Murdock, B. Paul, John M. Roberts, R. R. Sarbin, Pauline S. Sears, M. Brewster Smith, R. L. Solomon, John W. Thibaut, and John W. M. Whiting.

sion (Lambert, Triandis, and Wolf, 1959; Triandis and Lambert, 1961), and John Whiting worked on measures of guilt and other mechanisms of internalized controls (Burton and Whiting, 1961).

During June and July of 1954, a Social Science Research Council Summer Conference was held at the Laboratory of Human Development at Harvard. All the research personnel, with the aid of David Aberle of Michigan, Alfred Baldwin and James J. Gibson of Cornell, and Robert Sears of Stanford, wrote the *Field Guide for a Study of Socialization in Five Societies.** This guide appears as Volume 1 of the six culture series. It presents in detail the research plan, the hypotheses to be tested, and the research instruments agreed on by the field teams and the senior investigators. The reader should study this volume in order to understand the content and organization of the monographs and the methods employed in data collection. The theoretical background and the intellectual history of the project are presented in the preface by John W. M. Whiting.†

The five original field teams started work in the fall of 1954 and spent from 6 to 14 months in the field. Although the original design of the study called for a sample of societies whose culture had already been studied by ethnologists, the temperament and motivation of young anthropologists were such that they tended to choose groups who are relatively unknown and who, often from some personal reason, appealed to their interests. The actual groups chosen represent a compromise between the advantages of previous coverage and these personal interests, and also provide the great range of differences desired by the project planners.

Thomas and Hatsumi Maretzki chose the village of Taira on the northeast coast of Okinawa, the largest of the Ryukyu Islands in the Pacific. At the time, Thomas Maretzki was an advanced graduate student in the Anthropology Department at Yale University. Hatsumi Maretzki, a graduate of the University of Hawaii, was on the staff of the Gesell Institute Nursery School. Thomas Maretzki is now an associate professor of anthropology at the University of Hawaii.

Leigh Minturn worked with a group of families of the Rājpūt caste in the town of Khalapur in Uttar Pradesh in northern India. Unmarried at the time of the study, she used the facilities of Morris Opler's Cornell field station in Khalapur which then was directed by John Hitchcock, who collaborated with her in the study. Leigh Min-

---

* Published in mimeographed form by the Laboratory of Human Development, Harvard University, 1954.

† See also, Lambert, W. W., 1960.

turn received her doctorate from the Social Relations Department of Radcliffe College and Harvard University, and was, at the time of the study, a research associate at Cornell University. She is now an associate professor of psychology at the University of Illinois. John Hitchcock received his doctorate in anthropology from Cornell University and is at present an associate professor of anthropology at University of California, Los Angeles.

William and Corinne Nydegger chose a group of Ilocano-speaking families living in hamlets in northern Luzon in the Philippines. At the time of the study, William Nydegger was an advanced graduate student at Cornell University. His wife had done graduate work in anthropology at the University of Wisconsin. William Nydegger is now an associate professor of anthropology at Pennsylvania State University.

A. Kimball and Romaine Romney chose a group of families in the Mixtecan barrio of Santo Domingo in the town of Juxtlahuaca in Oaxaca State, Mexico. At the time of the study, A. Kimball Romney was an advanced graduate student at Harvard University. His wife attended the University of Colorado. A. Kimball Romney is now an associate professor of anthropology at Stanford University.

John and Ann Fischer agreed to take on the task of establishing bench marks for comparison by studying a group of mothers in the United States. They moved into a neighborhood in Orchard Town in New England. John Fischer, who has a doctorate in social relations from Harvard University, was at the time of the study an assistant professor at Harvard and his wife Ann was an advanced graduate student in anthropology. John Fischer is at present a professor of anthropology at Tulane University and his wife is an associate professor of anthropology at the same university. When they undertook the study, the Fischers had just returned from three years in the Caroline Islands in the Pacific where John Fischer had served as district anthropologist and as native affairs officer on the islands of Truk and Ponape in Micronesia. During this time, Ann Fischer was gathering material on child rearing in Truk; on the basis of this work she received her doctorate from Harvard.

In 1955 a sixth team, Robert and Barbara LeVine, left for Kenya, Africa where they studied a group of homesteads in the Kisii Highlands of South Nyanza District. They were financed by a Ford Foundation fellowship and a National Science Foundation predoctoral fellowship. At the time of the study Robert LeVine was an advanced graduate student in the department of social relations at Harvard University. Barbara LeVine was a graduate student of psychology at

Boston University. She subsequently received a doctorate in social psychology from Northwestern University. Now Barbara Lloyd, she is a lecturer in social psychology at the University of Birmingham in England. Robert LeVine is at present an associate professor of anthropology in the Committee on Human Development, University of Chicago.

To help insure comparability of data, a central clearing house was set up at the Laboratory of Human Development under the supervision of Beatrice B. Whiting, a Yale-trained anthropologist who was a research associate at the Laboratory of Human Development at Harvard. Field notes were mailed in periodically and field problems were discussed by correspondence.

The research design, agreed on by all the field teams, was set up to measure as accurately as possible the child-training practices and the hypothesized individual and cultural differences in personality, especially in the areas of aggression, dependency, and the internalization of various mechanisms of behavior control—areas of special theoretical interest to the senior investigators at Cornell, Yale, and Harvard universities, respectively. Previous research had been done in these areas at the Institute of Human Relations at Yale, at the Iowa Child Welfare Station under the direction of Robert Sears, and subsequently at the Laboratory of Human Development at Harvard University. The research conducted at Iowa and Harvard focused on a study of individual differences among groups of mothers and children in Iowa, Massachusetts, and in three different cultural groups in the Southwest (Sears, Whiting, Nowlis, and Sears, 1953; Whiting, Chasdi, Antonovsky, and Ayres, in press).

In designing the field research reported in this volume, an attempt has been made to assess individual as well as cultural differences. This is one of the unique aspects of the design. The hope was to test hypotheses about the relations of child-rearing practices and consequent personality, both intraculturally and cross-culturally. In the first instance, 24 mothers in each society were studied as individuals in their relationship to one of their children, and each of the 24 children (ages 3 to 10) was observed and interviewed in a standard manner in the hope of detecting behavioral and personality differences. (The mother interviews, child interviews, child T.A.T.'s, and the description of the observations of the children used in the study can be found in Chapter 5 of the *Field Guide for the Study of Socialization.*) The cross-cultural measures included material on child-training practices and also religious beliefs, theories of disease, recreational activities, and so on, collected by standard ethnographic techniques. The outlines for studying these are to be found in Chapter 2 of the *Field Guide for the Study of Socialization.*

A word should be said here about the nature of the social unit each field team chose to study. It was decided to choose a group large enough to yield an adequate sample of individual families. For our design this meant that a group of at least 50 families would be needed to draw our sample of 24, since at least half the families would have grown-up children, children under 3, or no children at all. On the other hand, we wanted a group who knew each other and shared beliefs, values, and practices so that it would be possible to use ethnographic techniques in collecting data and in describing certain aspects of the daily life in cultural terms. The techniques used to locate the Primary Social Unit (P.S.U.) are described in detail in the *Field Guide for the Study of Socialization,* Chapter 6.

In Taira, Okinawa, the Maretzkis visited 63 households in the central part of town and recorded the relationships among the occupants and their kin. The census included about 330 individuals, 83 of which were children under the age of 11.

In Khalapur, India, Leigh Minturn gathered census material in 38 courtyards; all were owned by members of the Rājpūt caste who constitute 40% of the total population of 5000. The courtyards are in a neighborhood inhabited exclusively by members of the Rājpūt caste; the area is bounded on two sides by a river and fields and is separated from the rest of the town on the third side by a temple, school, and meeting house and by a street occupied by another caste group, and on the fourth by a patti division line. (Khalapur is divided into seven political units or pattis.)

In Juxtlahuaca, a town of 3600, the Romneys made a census of 31 courtyards in the Mixtecan barrio of Santo Domingo. This section is separated from the rest of the town, which is inhabited by Spanish-speaking ladinos, by a deep barranca. The census of 31 courtyards included 90 children under 11 years of age.

In Orchard Town, population 5000, a census was made of 42 households, most of them on three adjoining streets in North Village, which has a population of 1000 and is one of the three centers of the town. The families participated together in P.T.A., school functions, women's clubs, and church, as well as in local politics. There were 83 children under 11 in the sample.

In the barrio of Tarong, Luzon, it was necessary to make a census of six adjacent hamlets before a sample of 24 children of the right age could be drawn. The barrio encompasses an area of about two square miles of land crosscut by steep ridges and valleys. The hamlets consisted of from 3 to 17 families. The sample was drawn from 58 families who had 76 children under 11 years of age. The genealogical material collected by the Nydeggers indicates that all but six of the 61 families in the barrio were descended from seven families who settled the area around 1860 (Minturn and Lambert, 1964, p. 18).

In Nyansongo, 18 contiguous homesteads were visited. The families in these homesteads all belong to one clan, and neighboring homesteads often belong to the same patrilineage. The census from which the sample was drawn included 208 individuals of whom 92 were children under 11.

In each of the six societies all the families knew each other and associated at certain times during the year and presumably met our criterion of sharing basic cultural values. If I were to judge the societies on the degree of intimacy of the mothers of the total P.S.U., I would rank the families in Taira as most intimate and those in Juxtlahuaca second. In the other societies there is intimacy in subgroups but not in the entire P.S.U. Although the Khalapur families live close to one another, the women are confined to courtyards, and most of their everyday contacts are limited to women in the same block who can be visited by crossing roof tops.

Women in groups of homesteads in Nyansongo are members of cooperative work teams and hence are on intimate terms with one another. There were three such work groups in the sample. The members of each belonged to the same subclan. Hamlet groups in Tarong are very intimate, especially when families face on the same yard. Visiting, kin ties, and a central school all unite the members of the P.S.U.

The Orchard Town mothers seem to be the least intimate in the sample, although they knew one another by name and knew the names of one another's children.

The P.S.U. groups are defined and selected to maximize the homogeneity which is essential for the use of standard ethnographic techniques. In gathering the background material and much of the material on socialization, the field teams used informants and participant observation. In areas that were not covered by standardized instruments, the data presented in the ethnographies is often based on a combination of discussion with from four to eight informants checked by observation of the daily life of the group. All the field teams lived in the communities they studied for the better part of a year or longer. Three of the field teams had children who played with the sample children. All the ethnographers visited the houses daily, participated in community activities, and became socialized in the habits of the group.

For the individual measures, 24 children were selected from the census material sent in by the field teams according to the following criteria: the sample consisted of four sex-age groups, six boys and six girls from 3-to-5 years of age and an equal number from 7-to-10 years of age.* To maximize the independence of cases, no more than one child was selected from each family. The sample mothers were interviewed and the children interviewed and observed in a standard manner for 12 five-minute periods.

Implicit in the research design is a general concept of the relation of personality to culture, which may be presented as follows: the ecology of an area determines the maintenance systems, which include basic economy and the most elementary variables of social structure. In other words, the type of crops grown, the presence or absence of herding, fishing, and so on, depend on the nature of the terrain, the temperature and amount of rainfall, and the location of the area vis-à-vis centers of invention and diffusion. These basic conditions partly determine the arrangement of people in space, the type of houses, and household composition. These in turn set the limits for child-rearing practices. The basic innate needs of both children and parents must be met within this framework.

It is obvious that ecology does no more than determine gross limits for the social structure. Within these limits the nature of the composition of households, neighborhoods, and other social groups will lead to variance in child training. Whether or not a grandmother lives in the house, or whether other relatives are close at hand, will influence a mother's behavior toward her child.

We assume that different patterns of child rearing will lead to differences in the personality of children and thus to differences in adult personality. Since personality may only be inferred, the problem of measurement is difficult on both the individual and the cultural levels. Individual children may be given tests of various kinds, interviewed, or observed. On a cultural level, we may analyze the patterning of child or adult behavior, for example, the games and recreational activity, the rituals or ceremonial life, or we may assess beliefs about the supernatural, theories of disease, or popular folk tales in terms of personality dimensions.

---

* The LeVines' sample was aberrant. They studied six sex-age groups consisting of four children each. They included a group 10-to-14 years of age since they wanted to follow the children through initiation. The Romneys' sample of older children was limited to five girls and five boys 7-to-10 years old.

Chart I indicates this conceptual system in a simple manner. To summarize the conceptual background in another way, the researchers viewed ecology, economics, and social and political organization as largely determining the behavior of the agents of child rearing. They viewed child behavior as an index of child personality and saw adult behavior, beliefs, and values as indices of adult personality. The causal relationships implied in this scheme are open to discussion. Such discussions, with the knowledge available at present, ultimately end with a problem similar to that of the priority of the chicken or the egg.

A word should be said about the type of ecology and economy represented in the sample. Five of the six cultures are agricultural. There are no fishing or hunting and gathering economies, nor are there pastoral people. With the exception of Orchard Town, most of the men in the six societies are farmers. In Tarong, Philippines and in Taira, Okinawa, the most important staple crop is wet rice. In Juxtlahuaca, Mexico and in Nyansongo, Kenya, corn is the important staple. In the latter, eleusine, a grain, is also important. In Khalapur, wheat and other grains are the main food crops.

Chart I   The Relation of Personality to Culture

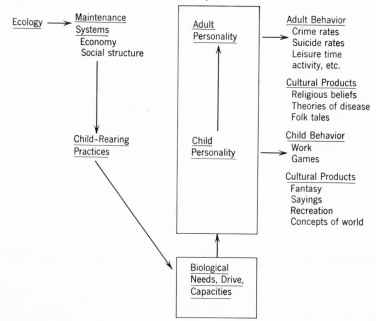

The ecology of the areas, however, makes the farming techniques different: in Taira and Tarong, men and women work together in the fields; in Khalapur and Juxtlahuaca only men work in the fields; in Nyansongo, with the exception of ploughing and building fences, all the agricultural work is done by women. An important variable in determining the amount of agricultural work women do is the distance of the gardens and fields from the dwellings. The gardens are closest in Nyansongo and Tarong, furthest away in Juxtlahuaca and Khalapur. Every Nyansongo woman has gardens close to her house, and she and a group of women who are members of her cooperative work group are responsible for all the gardening. In Tarong the fields and paddies lie directly below the houses which are built on the ridges. The town Juxtlahuaca is situated in a long, narrow river valley. Most of the cornfields near the town and in the valley belong to the ladinos in the Mexican part of town. The Mixtecans' main fields are usually a half-hour walk from home on the slopes of the mountains which follow the river valley. Women do not work in the fields in Juxtlahuaca. Clearing the mountain gardens is done by cutting the trees and undergrowth and burning it off, a technique called slash and burn agriculture. Khalapur is surrounded by fields that are a 15-to-20-minute walk from the courtyards. As in Juxtlahuaca, the Rājpūt women do not work in the fields; however, their enforced seclusion as married women would make such work impossible even if the fields were closer by. In Taira the rice paddies are also on the outskirts of the town. They are closer at hand, however, than are the fields in Khalapur and Juxtlahuaca, although not so close as are the paddies in Tarong. Both the Tarong and Taira women help in the fields, although it is my impression that the Taira women spend more time working in the gardens than the Tarong women do. It is interesting to note that, in the five agricultural societies, the women do more gardening work when the gardens are nearby. It also appears that in rice cultures women are especially good at transplanting the young shoots, a backbreaking and fussy job which requires manual dexterity and patience. Women do not work when slash and burn techniques are use. In all the five societies, men do whatever plowing is done. Buffaloes are used as draft animals in Khalapur, India, the carabao in Tarong, Philippines, and oxen in Juxtlahuaca, Mexico and in Nyansongo, Africa. In Taira, Okinawa there are few large animals. Because Nyansongo families cannot afford to hire ploughs, the women prepare the soil with hoes.

If the model of the influence of the maintenance systems on child rearing is correct, the amount of time and effort women exert in agricultural work is one of the several ecological and economic variables which influence their child-training techniques. The amount of time the fathers spend in the agricultural work and the distance of the fields from the house will influence the amount of time men spend around the house and the amount of time the children see them.

The majority of the families in Nyansongo in Kenya, in Tarong in the Philippines, and in Khalapur, India have large animals which must be watered and pastured. There are no adequate fences in any of these three societies, so humans must see that the cattle do not get into crops. This is done either by tethering the animals, the technique employed by the Tarongans, or by employing a herd boy when the cows are in pasture, the technique used by the Nyansongo and by the Rājpūts of Khalapur. The latter keep the cattle in pens adjoining the courtyards for much of the day and bring fodder into town. The Nyansongo shut the cattle up only at night. During the day, young boys or occasionally younger girls tend the herds. Where the herding technique is used, children are important in the economy and their negligence may ruin the crops essential for the food supply. As a consequence, training in responsibility is early and irresponsibility is severely punished.* Although there are sheep, goats, and burros in Juxtlahuaca, only a few of the families in the sample owned these animals. Here also herdboys are used.

Besides doing whatever agricultural work is expected, some of the women are involved in other economic pursuits. Most of the sample mothers in Taira helped their husbands in lumbering, carrying faggots down from the mountains and bundling them for sale. Some of the Juxtlahuacan mothers cooked for the markets. Some of the Tarongan and Nyansongo women occasionally sold surplus vegetables in the markets. In Orchard Town some women worked outside the home at wage-earning jobs. Only the Rājpūt women had no possible way of earning money.

In sum, the amount of work, excluding child care and housework, required of women varies with the economy and ecology. The Nyansongo women have the heaviest work load, the Orchard Town and Rājpūt mothers the lightest. The Taira and Tarong women seem to rank second and third in economic work load, the Juxtlahuaca fourth. The burden of housework and child care also varies. Here comparisons are difficult, and there are several factors that should be considered. Technological development in the processing of food and in the procurement of water and fuel is one of the determinants of the number

* See Barry, Child, and Bacon, 1959 for a discussion of responsibility training in economies having large animals. The authors interpret the relationship in terms of the amount of property accumulated and owned by members of a society.

of hours a woman spends in cooking and cleaning. For example, the
women in Tarong, Philippines, must pound their own rice whereas the
women in Taira take theirs to a mill to be processed. Both the Rājpūt
women of Khalapur and the Juxtlahuacan women spend long hours
preparing grain for cooking. The Orchard Town mother certainly has
the easiest lot in this domain; furthermore, she alone has water and
fuel readily available in her kitchen.

A second factor that must be considered is the availability of help.
As will be described later, in the kin-based hamlet groups in Tarong,
Philippines, in the extended family courtyards in Juxtlahuaca, Mexico,
and in Khalapur, India, and in the stem family households in Taira,
Okinawa, other adult women are available to help with the daily
routine of living. In the Nyansongo homestead, there may be co-wives
and mothers-in-law within shouting distance. It should be noted, however, that the degree to which women help each other when they live
close by and are related varies. In our sample, the closest cooperation
between women occurs in Tarong, Philippines; here the kin group is
often bilateral and a woman has her own relatives as well as her
husband's close at hand. Similarly, in Juxtlahuaca a woman may have
her own relatives nearby to help. Affinal relatives seem to be less
predictably helpful. In Khalapur the mothers report that they receive
little or no help from their sisters- and mothers-in-law, although these
relatives are at hand in emergencies.*

In Nyansongo homesteads the cooperation between co-wives varies
with the personality, with the difference in age of the wives, and with
the executive ability of the husband. It appears that when the second
wife is considerably younger than the senior wife, there is more likely
to be cooperation. Most Nyansongo mothers, however, use children,
usually siblings or cousins, between the ages of 5 and 8 to take over
the care of their infants, and these children are the constant com-
panions of their little charges until they can walk and travel with the
rest of the children. The Taira mother who is lucky enough to have a
mother-in-law or her own mother living in the house receives help with
the daily care of her infant. The Orchard Town mother, in contrast
to the mothers in the other five societies, has the least help. She can
hire baby-sitters, but in general she seldom does so. Even when her own
mother or her husband's mother lives in the same town, or even next
door, she is not in the habit of asking them to do more than occasional
baby-sitting.

---

* It should be noted that the Rājpūt mothers have outside help from sweepers,
washers, and water carriers who do some of the daily housework.

Even in child care, however, it should be noted that technological development is important. In our sample, for example, only the Orchard Town mother has a baby carriage. In all the other societies infants must be carried, and children are used in lieu of carriages. Similarly, there are no playpens or high chairs to confine the infant safely while the mother works.

Still a further dimension of comparison is the degree of loneliness of mothers. It is here that the Orchard Town mother is unique: she spends most of her day in the company of her children, isolated from other adults. This is especially true in winter, when it is an effort to bundle up the family and go on a visit.

Associated with loneliness is boredom, and here the Orchard Town mother is similar to the Rājpūt mother in Khalapur who is confined to the courtyard day after day. Both enjoy seeing and talking to someone new and look forward to any breaks in the monotony of the daily routine. Although the Rājpūt mothers usually have adult companionship, they cannot wander downtown or break the monotony either by watching people interact on television or by reading about them in books.

As suggested earlier, the climate influences daily living routine and arrangements in many ways. Children react to excessive heat and cold and grow restive if continuous rains confine them to the dwelling. In all the societies there are days when the temperature is uncomfortably cool (see Chart II). During November through March children may feel cold in the early morning in Juxtlahuaca, Mexico. In June, July, August, and September the nights may be uncomfortably cool in Nyansongo, Kenya. In both of these societies and in Khalapur, India, winter nights probably seem colder than they actually are because of the diurnal variation which averages over 25 degrees. Orchard Town, U.S.A., has by far the most prolonged period of cold and the most days with temperatures that drop below freezing. However, it has insulated buildings and central heating; the children have special winter clothes and hence probably suffer less from the cold than any of the other children in the sample. On the other hand, the Orchard Town mother has to struggle with snowsuits and boots and would often rather stay home than face the task of dressing and undressing children and walking or driving through the snow and ice. She is afraid to leave her children at home alone, even for short periods of time, lest faulty heating equipment set fire to the house. During the winter months the radio broadcasts almost daily the names of small children who have burned to death in their homes. The seasonal contrast in the routine of living is greater in Orchard Town than in any of the other societies.

Chart II   Climatic Conditions for the Six Societies[a]

SOCIETY	NYANSONGO	JUXTLA-HUACA	KHALAPUR	ORCHARD TOWN	TARONG	TAIRA
Weather Station						
Weather Station	Eldoret	Mexico City	New Delhi	Boston	Aparri	Naha
Observed Period	1930–1945	not given	1866–1943	1870–1949	1928–1937	1891–1935
Temperature						
Hottest month	March	April	June	July	April	July
Absolute high	85°	90°	115°	104°	101°	96°
Daily Range	79–50°	77–51°	102–83°	80–63°	90–73°	89–77°
Coldest month	December	January	January	February	December	February
Absolute low	37°	27°	31°	–18°	59°	41°
Daily Range	76–49°	66–42°	70–44°	37–21°	81–70°	67–55°
Precipitation						
Average yearly fall	40.5 in.	29.4 in.	25.2 in.	40.8 in.	89.5 in.	82.8 in.
Number of months with more than 14 days of rain	3	5	0	0	3	0
Number of months with fewer than 7 days of rain	5	4	10	0	2	0

[a] The material for this table is taken from a report of the Meteorological Office of the British Air Ministry, 1960. The weather stations with the nearest latitude and altitude to the field site were selected.

The sharpest contrast in the weather occurs in Khalapur, where the long periods of heat and drought make the rains in June, July, and August dramatic. Although the actual number of rainy days, even during these months is few (average eight days), the winds that accompany the rains and the intense heat which precedes them in April and May make the seasonal variation striking.

In the other societies it rains frequently throughout the year. But a rainy day ordinarily confines children to their houses only in Orchard Town where precipitation during two-thirds of the year may be accompanied by cold weather. Orchard Town children tend to associate rain with being forced to stay indoors. The rainy season in Juxtlahuaca, which lasts from June through September, can be cold and unpleasant. It rains over 20 days in each of these months and 27 days in two of them (July and August), and the temperature during the same period often falls below 50 degrees. The rainfall, however, is usually a drizzle and does not seem to upset the daily routine so much as the infrequent downpours in Khalapur.

Ecology and economy affect the life of children and their parents in another important way—they partly determine the arrangement of dwellings. The number of people who live in a household, the number of generations which interact daily, the distance between households, and the nature and amount of shared work and play space are factors that influence both the training of a child and his daily experiences.

Chart III shows the composition of households in the six societies. It can be seen that half of the households in Taira, Okinawa include at least one grandparent. It is customary for one son, preferably the oldest, to stay on after his marriage to care for his parents. In Khalapur, India, the majority of the households consist of a man and a woman and their married sons and children or married brothers and their children. In Nyansongo, Kenya, half of the men are polygynists and their wives have separate huts.

Chart III also indicates the average number of adult males, females, and children per household, the extended courtyards in Khalapur having the most people, Orchard Town the fewest. Note that the houses in Nyansongo may have only a woman if her husband is a polygynist who rotates between the huts of his wives. The households have, however, on an average as many children as the extended families in Khalapur. In sum, Nyansongo women have more children than any of the other women in the sample.

Chart IV gives the frequency of the groups whose houses face on an area which the occupants use in common. For the Nyansongo it indicates the people who share a homestead (the people included in these

Chart III Household Composition

	TAIRA	TARONG	KHALAPUR	JUXTLAHUACA	ORCHARD TOWN	NYANSONGO
Nuclear Husband, wife and child. May include siblings of husband or wife	11	19	8	18	23	6
Stem Nuclear family plus 1 or 2 parents of husband or wife	12	3	3	3	1	0
Stem plus Married Brother or married cousins. May include parents' siblings	0	0	7	0	0	0
Extended Lineal Nuclear family plus married children and/or married brothers and/or cousins and their children	1	2	6	0	0	0
Polygynous One wife and her children per house	0	0	0	0	0	8
Other	0	0	0	1	0	2
Average number of adult males	1.3	1.4	2.6	1.3	1.0	.87
Average number of adult females	1.8	1.7	2.4	1.2	1.0	1.0
Average number of children	3.5	3.5	5.7	4.0	2.8	5.8

Chart IV Courtyard Composition of Groups Larger than the Household Sharing Intimate Space

	TAIRA	TARONG	KHALAPUR	JUXTLAHUACA	ORCHARD TOWN	NYANSONGO
Households Do not share a yard with another household	23	5	21	5	21	4[a]
Stem Share a yard with one or both parents of husband or wife (who have their own house)	1	3	0	3	3	0
Extended Share a yard with parents of husband or wife and/or aunt or uncle plus married brothers and/or sisters and/or married cousins of husband or wife	0	12	0	6	0	1
Collateral Share a yard with brothers and/or sisters of husband or wife	0	3	0	6	0	0
Collateral Extended Share a yard with married brothers and/or sisters and married children and/or married nephews and nieces of husband and/or wife	0	0	3[b]	2	0	0
Non-kin Share a yard with non-kin	0	1	0	0	0	0
Polygynous Co-wives share a yard	0	0	0	0	0	6
Extended Polygynous Share a yard with married brothers of husband plus husband's parents and/or husband's mothers co-wives and married half brothers	0	0	0	0	0	5
Average number of adult males	1.4	3.2	2.9	2.9	1.1	2.1
Average number of adult females	1.8	4.3	2.6	3.0	1.2	3.2
Average number of children	3.9	7.9	5.9	6.7	2.8	7.1
Total	7.1	15.4	11.4	12.6	5.1	12.4

[a] Includes one polygynous homestead where huts of two wives are far apart and there is tension between the wives.
[b] Includes married first cousins and their children.

units interact daily in an intimate fashion). In Juxtlahuaca the houses face on a private courtyard; in Tarong they surround a yard. Tarong has the greatest number of people who interact on this level of intimacy, and Juxtlahuaca and Nyansongo units are similar in size. Taira and Orchard Town have, on an average, two fewer adults per unit.

As mentioned earlier, the household and dwelling units partly determine the amount of adult help a mother has in raising her children. Our theoretical paradigm suggests, then, that the combined factors of a mother's economic role and the people with whom she lives influence her patterns of child rearing. The first test of hypotheses related to this paradigm are presented in *Mothers of Six Cultures* by Leigh Minturn and William Lambert (1964). Further tests of the hypotheses will appear in a forthcoming volume on the behavior of the children.

The salience of the father in infancy and childhood is another variable that affects the personality development of the society. For a discussion of the relative salience of the father and hypothesized consequent effects on aggressive behavior, see Beatrice Whiting's "Sex Identity and Crimes of Violence: a Comparative study."

Six of the volumes in this series are monographs of each of the six societies. The outline for each is organized around the conceptual system just presented. There are two main parts: one, a description of the adult world into which the child is born—*the ethnographic background*; the second, an account of how the child is trained—*child training*. In Part I, each account starts with a description of the environment and the local setting, including the village plan, the houses, and their interior arrangements. Then the daily routine of living and the economic pursuits of men and women are described. A chapter on social structure follows. In other words, these chapters describe the maintenance system that set the stage for child rearing. The selection of material for the remainder of Part I is also theoretically determined and includes descriptions of either adult behavior or the cultural products that seem to be the best indices of adult personality.

To explain the selection of behavior and cultural products, we must return to the discussion of the dimensions of personality selected for study by the senior investigators. As noted, the hypotheses to be tested focused on aggression, dependency, and the internalization of various mechanisms of behavior control. William Lambert and the Cornell group, because of previous research, were most interested in aggression, Irvin Child in dependency, and John Whiting and the Laboratory of Human Development in the development of internal controls that have been variously labeled as guilt, conscience, and superego.

It was the conviction of the researchers that the areas of study had to be limited and clearly defined if standardized material was to be collected. Chapter 1 of the *Field Guide for the Study of Socialization* is a description of the "systems" of behavior which were chosen for study and the hypotheses which the investigators hoped to test. Although it is impossible to include a detailed description of the theory in this introduction, it is necessary to present at least a summary of the behavior systems and the nature of the hypotheses.*

The nine behavioral systems include succorance, nurturance, self-reliance, achievement, responsibility, obedience, dominance, sociability, and aggression. In the most general terms, succorance is defined as asking others for help; nurturance, as giving help or emotional support; self-reliance, as doing things for oneself; achievement, as striving to meet internal standards of excellence; responsibility, as performing one's expected role duties; obedience, as attempting to meet the demands of others; dominance, as attempting to change the behavior of others; sociability, as making friendly approaches to other individuals; aggression, as hurting others. It was assumed that each of these systems of behavior would exist in some recognizable form and degree in every society and could best be identified by people's responses to specific universal situations. For example, whether an individual who encountered difficulty asked for help or solved the problem himself would indicate the relative strength of his succorance or, in contrast, his self-reliance. A measure of nurturance would be the frequency of the spontaneous giving of help, the reaction to requests for help, or the perception that others need help.

Returning to the monographs, our descriptions of the adult culture of each society include material which we consider relevant to these nine behavior systems.

A chapter on social control is included in each monograph to give information about the frequency of brawls, fights, crimes, and other conflicts and to describe the techniques which the society has devised either for preventing such conflicts from occurring or for stopping existing conflict. This material gives comparative indices of the expressed aggression of the adults and the existence and type of internalized controls. It will be noted, for example, that the incidence of rape is high in Nyansongo, that litigation is frequent in Khalapur and Nyansongo, and that there are few cases of physical violence in either Taira or Juxtlahuaca.

* For a full discussion of behavior systems see Child (1954).

The chapter on medical practices and theories of disease is included because variations in such belief systems were found to be useful indices of personality in the cross-cultural study by Whiting and Child (1953) and in later studies by Whiting (1959). Similarly, the analysis of man's relation to the supernatural was fruitfully analyzed by Spiro and D'Andrade (1958), Whiting (1959), and Lambert, Triandis, and Wolf (1959). Mourning behavior and death ceremonies have also been studied cross-culturally (Friendly, 1956).

We hoped that an analysis of the use of leisure time might be made along dimensions relevant to the nine behavior systems. The man who prefers to be alone in his spare time would be rated less sociable than one who always seeks the company of others. The amount of teasing or playful wrestling in leisure settings, or even the amount of pleasure derived from cockfights, might be used to rate the degree of preoccupation with aggression. The amount of time spent practicing skills might indicate the need for achievement. Whether or not men seek the company of women, men and women, or only men is of interest in assessing personality. Similarly, we might rate a man's personality in terms of his preference for smoking, eating, talking, drinking, dancing, or playing games. The nature of popular games can be analyzed along lines suggested by Roberts, Bush, and Arth (1957).

Part II of the ethnographies is chronologically organized, beginning with pregnancy and childbirth and continuing through preadolescence. The time required to observe this age span made it impractical to systematically study the lives of the adolescent children. The only exception to this is the monograph on the Nyansongo group in Kenya. The LeVines were especially interested in the effect of initiation ceremonies on the Nyansongo boys and girls. For this reason, they selected three age groups for study: the 3-to-7-year-olds, the 7-to-10-year-olds, and the post-initiation boys and girls. The Nydeggers included a brief chapter on adolescence in their monograph on Tarong. The other field teams did not feel that they had enough knowledge to include such a description.

The age span covered in the individual chapters of the six descriptions of socialization differs; each division is made on the basis of the age groups and the transitions recognized by the members of the society. Thus in Khalapur, India, where socialization is not broken by clearly defined stages, there are only three chapters. In Taira, Okinawa, on the other hand, there are named stages and sharp transitions, and the Maretzkis have followed this pattern in describing socialization. Weaning from the breast and back is an abrupt change in an Okinawan child's life. The transition from kindergarten to school age is also clear and dramatic. Before reaching school age a child is "senseless" according to the mothers and cannot be properly trained.

Within these chapters an attempt has been made to cover the treatment of the nine behavior systems by the parent or parent surrogate and to study the child's response to socialization. Obviously, some of the behavior systems are not relevant in infancy. In general, the early chapters in the socialization section concentrate on the handling of succorance, the mother's early contact with the child, the number of other individuals who share in the early care of the child, and their responsiveness to the demands of the infant. Among the hypotheses advanced in the *Field Guide for the Study of Socialization,* several concern the consequence of indulgence in infancy. As stated: "Indulgence in infancy, a large number of nurturing agents, and mild transition from infantile indulgence into childhood will produce (1) a trustful attitude toward others, (2) general optimism, and (3) sociability." It is also stated that training with respect to succorance will tend to influence sociability.

We hope that, on the basis of the information presented in the chapters on infancy, the reader can compare the degree of indulgence in infancy and the number of nurturing agents. A comparison of weaning from the breast and from complete dependence on caretakers should make it possible to evaluate the severity of the transition. For the consequent measures, we may turn either to the description of the behavior of older children or to the behavior and belief systems of adults. Is it true that the Mixtecan child of Juxtlahuaca is comparatively more friendly and sociable in later life than the Nyansongan? In infancy, the Mixtecan is constantly held or carried close to the mother's body, and she responds relatively quickly to the infant's demands. The Nyansongon child is tended for periods of time by a less consistently responsive 5-to-8-year-old child. In adult life, are Mixtecans more optimistic and trustful than the Nyansongans?

With the onset of weaning, other behavior systems become important. Training for self-reliance and the associated punishment for succorance are universal problems, but the degree to which this new behavior is expected of 3-year-olds varies from one society to another. The Orchard Town 3-year-old is feeding and dressing himself, whereas the Khalapur Rājpūt child of the same age may still be dressed and fed by his mother. Similarly, as mentioned earlier, the abruptness of the shift in expected behavior varies. The handling of aggression against parents, siblings, and peers at this age-level is also a universal problem which all parents and socializers must face. Probably closely associated with this behavior system is training for obedience and respect.

The *Field Guide for the Study of Socialization* contains many hypotheses about the antecedents of aggressive behavior in children and adults and stresses the techniques used by parents in the handling of aggression as well as their behavior as models. Specifically, one hypothesis is that permissiveness on the part of parents for teasing behavior should be reflected in the increase of observable unprovoked aggressive behavior on the part of children and adults. Is it indeed true that the Tarongan child who is "playfully" teased by his parents and other adults from early childhood instigates aggressive behavior more frequently than a Rājpūt child whose parents do not "playfully" tease him?

A second hypothesis concerning the handling of aggression states that children will be less likely to retaliate against aggression if parents and socializing agents punish any expression of anger. Again, the Khalapur Rājpūt child whose mother dislikes all expression of emotion, even excessive joy, and the Mixtecan child of Juxtlahuaca who is taught that he will become sick and die if he eats while he is angry should be less aggressive when provoked than the children of Orchard Town.* It will be noted that a distinction is made between unprovoked and provoked aggression. A further distinction is made for instrumental aggression, when a person tends to select aggressive means for attaining his goals. Comparisons between the handling of aggression in childhood may also be used to explore hypotheses about the conditions that lead to the displacement of aggression to others, the use of fantasy to express anger, or the projection of one's own desires to hurt others. For an understanding of consequent measures, the reader may turn to theories of diseases and the nature of the supernatural. Theory predicts that the societies which punish aggression most severely project their anger into the supernatural world and believe in dangerous and malevolent beings or attribute superhuman evil capacity to humans and believe in sorcery or witchcraft. To date, the best socialization variable for predicting the belief in witches and sorcerers is a combination of polygyny and the severe punishment for sex and aggression (Whiting, 1959). Among our societies, the Nyansongans are the most ridden with belief in superhuman individuals. Their treatment of aggression is therefore of particular interest. It is also of interest to

---

* For further discussion of the hypotheses regarding aggression, see the *Field Guide for the Study of Socialization*, Chapter 1.

speculate whether there is some relation between the Tarongan parents' treatment of aggression and teasing behavior and their belief in whimsical spirits who must be avoided and not annoyed.

Each monograph on socialization also includes an extended section on techniques used by the socializing agent. Our theory stresses the importance of rewards and punishments for the specific types of acts included in the nine behavioral systems. We are interested in the differential effect of various types of rewards and punishments and the conditions under which they are administered. Rewards may be material, such as food or money, or immaterial, as love and acceptance or praise and prestige. Privileges may also be given as rewards. All types of rewards may be given to commend good behavior or to incite desired behavior. Punishments depend on two types of sanctions, injury or abandonment; these may have as referents several types of agents—parents or authority figures, peers, the self, or supernatural agents.

These rewards and punishments may be given for different reasons. The locus of evaluation may be a specific response of the child, some consequence of his action, or the child himself as a person. In other words, a child may be praised because he does a chore well, because he has helped his mother by doing the chore, or because he is a good boy.

Rewards and punishments may also be intrinsic to the environment. For example, in a terrain where there are delicious wild berries, being able to locate, pick, and eat the berries without aid from adults may reward self-reliance. Herding large animals may reward dominance. Hot, humid weather may discourage physical exertion.

The nature and strength of internal controls—mechanisms which keep an individual from breaking the rules of a society—are thought to be related to techniques and agents of socialization as well as to the strength of a child's identification with both parents (Whiting and Child, 1953; Whiting, 1960; Burton and Whiting, 1961; Bacon, Child, and Barry, 1963). To determine the strength of these internal controls, we hoped to observe the differences in children's behavior in the presence and absence of socializing agents. On a societal level, we predicted that when a boy's identification with the same sex parent is weak, there will be a higher incidence of crime (see B. Whiting, in press).

We expected to find that authority figures would be important sanction agents in the adult culture when there was marked differentiation of authority within the nuclear family, when discipline was carried out by or in the name of the head of the house, and when responsibility and obedience training were emphasized. We expected peers to be important agents when there was little differentiation of authority within the family, when the right of discipline was not stressed, and when self-reliance training was emphasized. If these hypotheses are correct, we would expect consequent differences in the social control systems.

For most of the societies, the age period from 6 to 10 emphasizes responsibility training. A comparison of the chores assigned to boys and girls during this period, of the rewards and punishments for good or bad performance or omission, is an index of the training in this behavior system. The age at which different types of chores are assigned gives a clue to the age at which a society considers a child to have "sense," to be capable of reason, and it indicates the beliefs about the nature of the learning process. It will be observed, for example, that the Khalapur Rājpūts believe that children learn primarily by observing; hence there is little direct instruction. One type of responsibility is training children to care for younger siblings, cousins, and neighbors. This training may start very early, as in Taira and Nyansongo, or may be late and unimportant, as in Orchard Town.

The size and composition of play groups and the attitudes of parents about friendliness are described for each age level. It was hypothesized that sociability would be related both to training in nurturance and to the treatment of succorance, but initial comparisons of children's observed behavior indicate that nurturance is probably more closely related to training for responsibility and dominance than to friendliness.

In planning the research, the senior investigators were also interested in discovering age and sex differences in behavior which might be universal (Barry, Bacon, and Child, 1957). Is it true, in spite of radically different treatment in infancy and early childhood in the six societies, that boys and adult men are always more aggressive physically than girls and women and that girls and women are always more affectionate than men? Are there regularities in behavior that hold across cultures? Does succorance always decrease with age and dominance always increase? We have tested these and other hypotheses using the behavioral measures derived from the systematic observation of the sample children (see *Field Guide for the Study of Socialization*, Chapter 1). The results will be published in the forthcoming volume on the *Behavior of Children in Six Cultures*. Preliminary findings do reveal universal sex-age difference. Although these questions cannot be answered from a comparison of the six societies alone, consistent age and sex differences should be followed up by further research.

Mothers in Six Cultures by Leigh Minturn and William Lambert (1964) presents the first perusal of many of the hypotheses just given.

The authors based their analysis on factor scores derived from ratings made on the mothers' answers to the standard interview on child-training practices (see *Field Guide for the Study of Socialization*, Chapter 5). For example, the mother's economic responsibility outside the house, the amount of help she received in caring for her infants and children, and the number of other adult women and their kin relationship are studied in relation to her use of praise or physical punishment, to her concern with training her children to be responsible and to help with daily chores, and to her attitudes toward her child's expression of aggression toward other children and toward herself. The authors discuss the rank order of the societies on these variables and the rank order correlation between these and other variables. They also consider the effect of ecological and demographic variables on the mother's deviation from the norms of her group.

The reader will be aware that in spite of the research design, the data are not always comparable; in the different areas studied, some monographs have better coverage than others. These variations result not only from the personalities, interests, and training of the field-workers but also from the nature of the culture of the society they chose to study.

Although these monographs concentrate on the material that the researchers felt was theoretically relevant, it is hoped that readers with different conceptual systems and different hypotheses concerning human behavior will find it possible to peruse the data with relevant comparisons in mind. Those who were concerned with the project have developed new insights and new hypotheses. Some of these can be explored, but for many the relevant data are not detailed enough and further studies must be conducted. We believe that the need for further studies is inevitable in the social sciences and that progress comes from being willing to state hypotheses, test them, derive new theories, and plan new research to test these.

We believe that the detailed comparison of six societies is useful for generating hypotheses about human behavior. To test hypotheses adequately, the social scientist must study predicted variation among individuals within societies as well as across a larger sample of societies.

In conclusion, we should like to acknowledge our indebtedness to many people and institutions for their advice and help. The opportunity to do the study was provided by the generous support of the Social Science Research Council and of the Behaviorial Science Division of the Ford Foundation, and by a United States Public Health Grant, M-1096.

Various faculty members at the three universities helped in designing and planning the research. A list of these and other contributors will be found at the beginning of this chapter, but we wish to express special gratitude to Robert R. Sears, Pauline Sears, Eleanor E. Maccoby, and Alfred L. Baldwin, who have continued to give valuable advice to the project.

While in the field, each of the teams was assisted by graduates of local universities and schools who acted not only as interpreters but also as informants and friends. The aid that these students gave was invaluable. We wish to thank Nariyuki Agarie, Gurdeep Jaspal, Simeon Nyaechae, John Okiamba, Felix Ombasa, Laurence Sagini, Sri Shyam Narain Singh, Taurino Singson, Muriel Eva Verbitsky Hunt, and Kiyoshi Yogi.

We are deeply grateful to all the staff and students of the Laboratory of Human Development of Harvard University who read and helped edit the monographs. Marilyn Johnson, Celia Kalberg, Dorothy Tao, and Susan Horton were particularly devoted assistants. We wish to express our appreciation to numerous other people for reading and commenting on some or all the monographs, especially Masanori Higa, Geraldine Kohlenberg, and Morris Opler.

We are especially indebted to the families in Nyansongo, Khalapur, Taira, Juxtlahuaca, Tarong, and Orchard Town, who were not only cooperative informants, but also helpful friends. We hope that the children we studied will become proud members of the adult world into which they were born and that these volumes will contribute to mutual understanding so that they may live in a friendlier world.

BEATRICE B. WHITING

Harvard University
September, 1965

BIBLIOGRAPHY

Air Ministry, Meteorological Office. *Tables of Temperature, Relative Humidity and Precipitation for the World.* London: Her Majesty's Stationery Office, 1960.

Bacon, Margaret K., Child, Irvin L., and Barry, Herbert III. A cross-cultural study of correlates of crime. *Journal of Abnormal and Social Psychology,* 1963, **66**, 291–300.

Barry, Herbert III, Bacon, Margaret K., and Child, Irvin L. A cross-cultural survey of some sex differences in socialization. *Journal of Abnormal and Social Psychology,* 1957, **55**, 327–332.

———, Child, Irvin L., and Bacon, Margaret K. Relation of child training to subsistence economy. *American Anthropologist,* 1959, **61**, 51–63.

Burton, Roger V. and Whiting, John W. M. The absent father and cross-sex identity. *Merrill-Palmer Quarterly,* 1961, **7**, 85–95.

Child, Irvin L. Socialization. In Gardner Lindzey (Ed.), *Handbook of Social Psychology*, vol. II. Cambridge, Mass.: Addison-Wesley, 1954.

Friendly, Joan P. A cross-cultural study of ascetic mourning behavior. Unpublished honors thesis, Radcliffe College, 1956.

Lambert, William W. Interpersonal Behavior. In P. H. Mussen (Ed.), *Handbook of Research Methods in Child Development*, Chapter 20, pp. 854–917. Wiley, New York: 1960.

————, Triandis, Leigh M., and Wolf, Margery. Some correlates of beliefs in the malevolence and benevolence of supernatural beings: a cross-cultural study. *Journal of Abnormal and Social Psychology*, 1959, **58**, 162–169.

Minturn, Leigh, Lambert, William W., et al., *Mothers of Six Cultures: antecedents of child rearing*. New York: Wiley, 1964.

Roberts, John M., Bush, R. R., and Arth, M. Dimensions of mastery in games. Stanford, Calif.: Ford Center for Advanced Study in the Behavioral Sciences, 1957 (mimeographed).

Sears, R. R., Whiting, John W. M., Nowlis, V., and Sears, P. S. Some child-rearing antecedents of aggression and dependency in young children. *Genetic Psychology Monograph*, 1953, **47**, 135–234.

Spiro, Melford E. and D'Andrade, Roy G. A cross-cultural study of some supernatural beliefs. *American Anthropologist*, 1958, **60**, 456–466.

Triandis, L. M. and Lambert, W. W. Sources of frustration and targets of aggression: a cross-cultural study. *Journal of Abnormal and Social Psychology*, 1961, **62**, 3, 640–648.

Whiting, Beatrice B. Sex identity conflict and physical violence: a comparative study. *American Anthropologist*, in press.

Whiting, John W. M. Sorcery, sin and the superego: a cross-cultural study of some mechanisms of social control. In *Nebraska Symposium on Motivation*, pp. 174–195. Lincoln: University of Nebraska Press, 1959.

————, Resource mediation and learning by identification. In I. Iscoe and H. Stevenson (Eds.), *Personality Development in Children*. Austin: University of Texas Press, 1960.

————, and Child, Irvin L. *Child Training and Personality: a cross-cultural study*. New Haven, Conn.: Yale University Press, 1953.

————, Chasdi, Eleanor M., Antonovsky, Helen F., and Ayres, Barbara C. The learning of values. In E. Z. Vogt (Ed.), *The Peoples of Rimrock*, Cambridge, Mass.: Harvard University Press, in press.

————, et al. *Field Manual for the Cross-Cultural Study of Child Rearing*. Social Science Research Council, New York, 1953.

————, et al. *Field Guide for a Study of Socialization*. Six Cultures Series, vol. 1. New York: Wiley, 1966.

About the Authors

A. Kimball Romney received his doctorate in anthropology from the Social Relations Department of Harvard University (1956). His wife Romaine attended the University of Colorado. The Romneys selected a Mixtecan barrio in the town of Juxtlahuaca in the province of Oaxaca in central Mexico. They had two children, Becky, aged 7 and Bobby, aged three, a third child was born in Oaxaca during their stay and spent the first months of her life being cared for by the women of the barrio. The baby has a Mixtecan name and Mixtecan godparents and is considered a member of the barrio. Two teenagers lived with the Romneys and helped both with the daily routine of living and with fieldwork. Romaine Romney had little opportunity after the first few months to do formal fieldwork, but spent her time with the other women marketing, cooking, attending church and fiestas, and caring for the young children. Bobby, a vigorous and active boy, was a source of fascination and pleasure to his less active and less boisterous Mixtecan friends. Becky did creditable fieldwork on her own. Muriel Eva Verbitsky, a graduate student at the University of Mexico, acted as an assistant to the Romneys and did most of the mother interviews and many of the standard observations of the children. Duane and Barbara Metzer, as well as Robert Ravicz, contributed to the work. The Romneys spent nine months in the field and returned the following summer. They lived in an adobe house which was specially built for them but was similar to the surrounding Mixtecan houses.

A. Kimball Romney is now a Professor in the Department of Social Relations at Harvard University. Muriel Eva Verbitsky Hunt received her doctorate in anthropology from the University of Chicago in 1963. She is now an instructor in the Social Science Department at the University of Chicago.

Contents

Part I

Ethnographic Background

Chapter 1

Setting and Overview

Santo Domingo barrio is part of the town of Juxtlahuaca in the state of Oaxaca, Mexico. The cultural heritage of the 600 barrio members we studied derives basically from the Mixtec Indians whose culture was flourishing in the area before the time of Christ.

The barrio itself is located on the site of a pre-Columbian Mixtec town and represents a continuation of many aspects of Mixtec culture up to the present. We know from documentary evidence that the first Spanish priest came into Juxtlahuaca in the 1620's and that six Spanish families took up permanent residence in 1636, at which time construction of the original Catholic church began.

Today the Mixtec-speaking peoples number approximately 250,000 and occupy an area of about 10,000 square miles in the north and west parts of the state of Oaxaca. We know from archaeological data that they have occupied this general area for at least 2000 years. In a number of respects, the impact of conquest was different in degree from other parts of Mexico. It occurred with little armed force, and there was relatively little compulsory emigration or labor in mines, for the rough terrain made exploitation uneconomical.

Although priests penetrated the area early in introducing religious changes, the basic subsistence patterns have been little affected. The addition of some fruits and vegetables was supplementary: maize, beans, and chile have remained the basic diet. Even the introduction of oxen and the plow have failed to affect greatly the pattern of land exploitation. Thus the intrusion of Spanish culture elements in the Mixtec area has involved little change in such features as land usage, subsistence patterns, residence, and certain aspects of village organization.

THE REGION

Mexico is a mountainous country with only some 7% of its land being described as level or rolling. The state of Oaxaca, lying at the juncture of the Eastern Sierra Madre and the Sierra of Oaxaca, is also mainly mountainous. The rugged terrain is cut by narrow river valleys whose slopes rise steeply to high peaks and ridges. The long summer rains make raging torrents out of the otherwise sluggish streams. Communities are consequently somewhat isolated from one another.

The state of Oaxaca is divided into 28 districts. Juxtlahuaca is a village or town located in the extreme west central part of the state (see map 1) and is the *cabecera* or head town, roughly equivalent to a county seat, of a district of the same name. The district is approximately 54 miles from north to south and 48 miles from east to west. This 3000 square miles is further divided into *municipios*. These *municipios* may be thought of as towns together with a large surrounding area inhabited by scattered hamlets and isolated families. Thus there is no land between *municipios,* for all the land and the people living on it belong to some *municipio.*

If viewed from above in three-dimensional perspective, the topography of the district is seen as a steep-sided valley shaped much like a tilted trough running from south to north with the lower end to the north. The sides are formed by mountain chains of over 10,000 feet, and the floor is comprised of the narrow valley of the Mixteco (or at this point, it is sometimes called the Juxtlahuaca) River, a valley that nowhere reaches 2 miles in width and that in most places is no wider than the river. The sides of the valley are cut by numerous steep-sided gullies

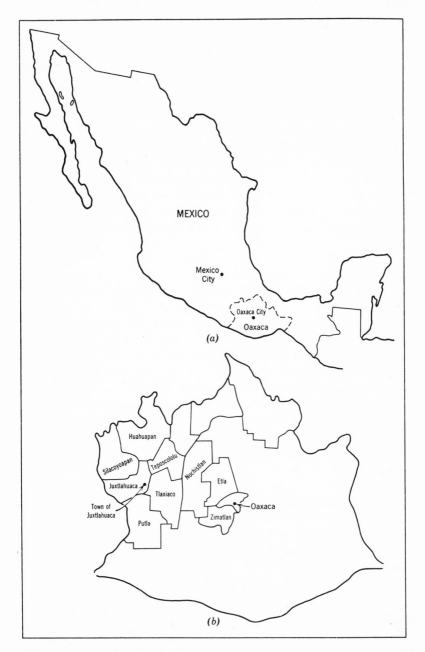

Map 1. (a) Map of Mexico showing state of Oaxaca. (b) State of Oaxaca showing Juxtlahuaca and surrounding districts.

and ravines cut by streams that drain the mountains. The town of Juxtlahuaca is located about 20 miles north of the southern head or origin of the valley at an altitude of 6500 feet at the confluence of two tributaries to the Mixteco River (see map 2). The only other town of any size in the district, Tecomastlahuaca, is located about 2 miles away near the junction of the Tecomastlahuaca River with the Mixteco River.

Juxtlahuaca, with a population of nearly 3600, and Tecomastlahuaca, with a population of about 2500, together with eight small villages of less than 500 each, numerous hamlets, and scattered families, bring the population of the *municipio* to about 30,000, with an average density of about ten people per square mile. Juxtlahuaca and Tecomastlahuaca are mostly Spanish speaking, although each contains a Mixtec-speaking *barrio* or community neighborhood. Otherwise, practically all the people in the district speak only an Indian dialect.

Map 2 shows the two main towns of the district. It is approximately 5 miles across the map, so that about 25 out of a total of 3000 square miles for the whole distirct is shown in the map. It takes about half an hour to walk from Juxtlahuaca to Tecomastlahuaca, or from Juxtlahuaca to Santa Rosa, while it takes about four to five hours to walk from the valley floor to the crests of the mountains, which are, of course, far out from the area shown by the map. It is also important to point out that much of the level ground in the district is shown in the map.

One enters the valley through the town of Huajuapan, a commercial center of the area that lies to the north on the Pan American highway between Mexico City and Oaxaca. Huajuapan is about 200 miles south of Mexico City and about 120 miles north of Oaxaca. There is a dirt road between Huajuapan and Juxtlahuaca that may be traversed only in the dry season in jeeps or very large trucks. The 65 miles between the two towns take about 14 hours of difficult driving. A similar, though less traveled, road joins Juxtlahuaca to the highway via Tlaxiaco.

During the rainy months, roughly May through September, both roads are impassable, the former lying in a river bed and the latter following a mountain ridge on which slides are frequent. An alternative method of entering the community is in small aircraft. A cleared field at the north end of town serves as a dry-season landing strip, but planes cannot land if the strip is muddy, and they do not fly on cloudy or rainy days. Hence, for some of July (when it may rain ten days or more) and virtually all of August and September (when it rains almost two thirds of the days) plane travel is impossible. Even during the dry months of October to May, the use of planes is limited by winds which rise every afternoon and continue with some force until well into the night.

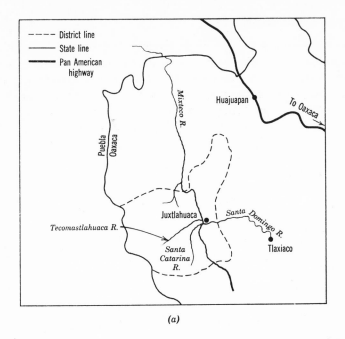

(a)

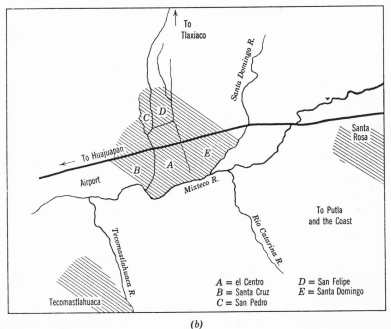

A = el Centro
B = Santa Cruz
C = San Pedro

D = San Felipe
E = Santa Domingo

(b)

Map 2. (a) *District of Juxtlahuaca showing town of Juxtlahuaca.* (b) *Town of Juxtlahuaca showing barrios and adjacent towns.*

5

In any case, the cost of a plane trip is prohibitive for many, and most of the Indian population travel, if at all, on foot.

Mean temperatures throughout the year vary only slightly as a result of the cloud cover in summer and the afternoon winds during the rest of the year. The warmest months are May, June, July, and August with lows of 50° F and highs of 86° F; the mean temperature being 70° F. The coldest part of the year is during December, January, and February, with lows of 32° F and highs of 86° F and a mean temperature of 60° F.

THE TOWN

Juxtlahuaca, then, lies in the widest section of the valley between the river and the mountains on the east. The road from Huajuapan, which skirts the landing strip, enters the town on the edge of the plaza. The large, whitewashed adobe church, built in 1633, is the first landmark one sees. Beyond the church to the south is the treeshaded town square or park containing two water fountains, several benches, and a circular speaking platform or *kiosco* that faces toward the *juzgado* or municipal buildings. These buildings house the administrative offices for the district as well as the jail and barracks for the local detachment of soldiers. The market, an open roofed structure, is located on the south side of the square, and Friday is market day. It is on Fridays that people from the several surrounding communities and hamlets come into town to trade their wares, and the market overflows into the cobblestoned streets around the square. A few traders from warmer areas carry fruits, coffee, nuts, and other products up from near the coast for this market day. Pottery, corn, fruits, beans, and innumerable other products are brought in by people from closer villages. Very little handicraft is found in the market. On any other day the market is confined to the covered structure, and the plaza is virtually empty.

Within a few blocks of the plaza, on the streets which converge on it, are the telegraph office, the post office, and the two schools (one federal and one private Catholic). A number of small general stores open onto these streets and sell canned and packaged foods, clothing, yard goods, and hardware. A vacant building is rented occasionally during the winter for showing of old Mexican movies. This section of town is called *el Centro,* the center. Around its edges lie the four *barrios* (el Centro itself is not considered to be a barrio). On map 2, el Centro is designated A, and the four barrios, Santa Cruz, Guadalupe, San Pedro, and Santo Domingo, are designated B, C, D, and E respectively. The people of el Centro are purely Spanish speaking and consider themselves superior to other residents of the town. Santa Cruz is also Spanish speaking and is composed of farmers and handicraft people only slightly lower in general prestige than people of el Centro, whom we shall call townspeople. Guadalupe is composed of very poor, Spanish-speaking people who have moved to Juxtlahuaca from surrounding Indian hamlets only within the last generation. They have very little land and live by making charcoal and working for low wages for townspeople. San Pedro, again, is Spanish speaking on the whole, although many also speak Mixteco. Many of its people are only one or two generations removed, culturally speaking, from being Indians. They are generally progressive and would rank above people in Guadalupe in prestige. Everyone in Santo Domingo, on the other hand, speaks Mixteco, although most also speak Spanish. Santo Domingo barrio contains approximately 600 people as compared to about 3000 for the rest of the town combined.

THE BARRIO

Santo Domingo barrio is composed entirely of Indians. They are distinguishable from Spanish-speaking townspeople, although not primarily by physical type, for both groups are relatively short and brown skinned with black hair which is naturally straight. (The town population does include a few blonds and redhaired people, but the Indian population does not.) The basis for the distinction is cultural rather than physical and is most clearly seen in language and dress.

Mixteco is the first language a barrio child learns and the only language some of the oldest barrio people speak. Most people between these extremes speak Spanish as well, but Mixteco is used at home and in most of the daily routine. Spanish is used when it is required—in dealings with the priest and nuns and with merchants in el Centro, none of whom know any Mixteco. Barrio meetings and all the events of the barrio fiestas are conducted in Mixteco, but if a non-Mixteco guest is present, the conversation will be carried on in Spanish as a courtesy. Schoolchildren are under pressure to use Spanish at school and frequently also use it at play. Children of preschool age, especially those who have no older siblings, hear Spanish much less and do not learn it until shortly before they are ready to enter school. However, young children who spend a great deal of time with an older sister who has learned Spanish begin to learn it from her, for she will often use it, except for expressions of endearment or warnings given under stress.

The typical, conservative costume of barrio men is homemade of coarse, white cotton material. It consists of a pair of trousers which reach to midcalf, where they are tied, and which are secured at the waist by wrapping and tying in back. They have neither buttons nor pockets, but a pocket for carrying money is improvised by tucking a small cotton bag into the waist band. The long-sleeved, collarless shirt has a concealed pocket on the inside left front in which are carried cigarettes or tobacco and sometimes folding money. Huaraches, a locally made leather sandal with heavy rubber sole, are worn on the feet. Every man has a sombrero. A plaid wool blanket or serape, sometimes with an opening cut for the head, is used for warmth outdoors in the early morning or at night. It also serves as a covering for sleeping.

Many barrio men have an alternative set of clothing, a shirt and pants made of a heavy cotton material and purchased ready-made. This costume, in fact, predominates except in wet weather, when frequent changes of clothing are necessary, but old men and very poor men wear only the typical costume. The trend toward this ready-made outfit is illustrated by the fact that only a small percentage of Indian boys wear the white cotton costume. In other respects, boys dress much like their fathers except that they do not always have huaraches. They wear no underclothing, although during the coldest part of the year they may wear two shirts. The boy's serape is made by cutting a wool or cotton blanket in half. A hat is not a necessary piece of clothing for boys, although most boys do have them. These sombreros are purchased new for the fiesta in July, and a child wears his hat as long as it lasts, but no new one is purchased until the following year. This may mean that a boy has no sombrero for the rainy season, in June and early July, for the fiesta is on July 24, and the new hat is purchased only a week or two before.

Indian women wear a hand-embroidered, white cotton blouse and a printed cotton skirt which reaches almost to the ground—both home-made. They cover their heads and shoulders as well as carry their infants with a rebozo, a long, dark blue cotton shawl. This rebozo and the characteristic way in which it is draped are the mark of a Mixteco woman throughout this part of the state. Women are traditionally barefoot. They carry money in a cotton bag tucked inside the blouse. Small loads are carried in handbaskets woven locally, and heavy loads are carried in a *tenate,* or carrying-basket, on a tumpline across the forehead. The hair is worn in braids which either hang down the back or are wrapped around the head. Earlobes are pierced for earrings, but not all women wear them. No make-up of any kind is worn.

Unlike the men's costume, the women's costume is worn by all adult barrio women without exception or alternative. However, a trend toward a ready-made costume for women is perhaps observable among children and adolescent girls. Little girls wear one-piece, knee-length dresses of printed cotton, often a slip, and sometimes panties, although the latter are not necessary for girls under 7. Like their mothers, they are barefoot and wear the rebozo whenever they are outdoors, regardless of the weather. Adolescent girls wear a knee-length printed cotton skirt with blouse (not embroidered) or a one-piece dress. However, the traditional costume is still the basis of the trousseau and is worn by all recently married girls.

The dress of barrio people provides them with relatively little protection against the elements. Children rarely have a change of clothing; when the clothing is drenched in a sudden rainstorm, the wet rebozo or serape is simply turned over or turned around rather than changed. Unless there is cooking in progress, there is no fire over which to dry wet clothing, and the child must often sleep in clothing still wet from a daytime shower. For many children the rebozo or serape is their only covering at night, even though it may often be quite cold. During the day the wind is chilling, especially if one is wet, and even during the dry season it may blow dust or dirt so hard that it is difficult to see across the street. Similarly, the rebozo may protect the head from direct exposure to the sun but is hot to wear in full sun. During the hottest part of the day the streets are almost deserted except for occasional playing children, and resting in the shade at this hour is not uncommon.

Santo Domingo is set off from the rest of the town by a clear geographical boundary. A deep *barranca* through which a stream runs lies at the southern end of town and separates it from el Centro. Santo Domingo is referred to locally as *the* barrio, and we shall adopt this practice. The barrio occupies about the same area as the remainder of the town, with the result that one sixth of the total population lives on onehalf the total land (see map 3).

The moment one crosses the natural boundary, the barranca, the distinctive features of the barrio become apparent. None of the barrio's streets is paved in any way except for an occasional pathway of stones. Two or three of them, those which lead across the barrio toward el Centro, are as wide as a road and flat. The others slope more or less sharply and are narrow, rocky, and cut by gullies. During the rainy season most of these become intermittent, muddy streams, and at planting time, water diverted from the river for irrigation runs down several streets from the hillside.

The houses along the streets are separated from each other by occasional cornfields or fields of alfalfa. Although some present a blank, windowless adobe wall, the back of a room that opens on the inner

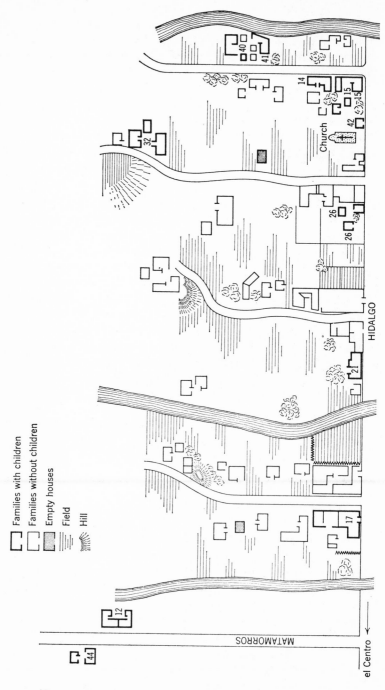

Families with children
Families without children
Empty houses
Field
Hill

MATAMORROS

HIDALGO

Church

el Centro

12

44

17

32

14
15
42

26
26

40
41

10

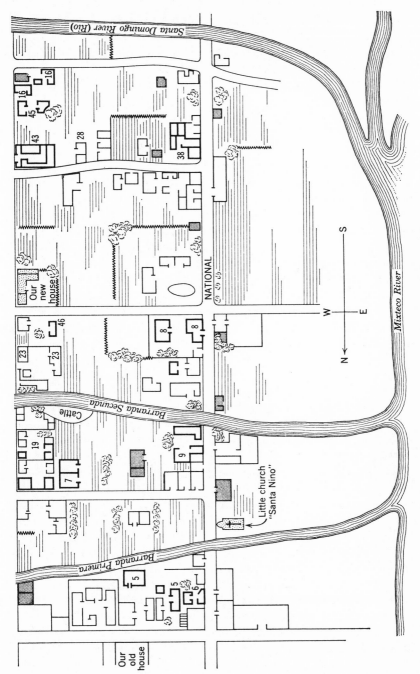

Map 3. Barrio of Santo Domingo, Juxtlahuaca, Oaxaca.

11

courtyard, most houses in the barrio are set back from the street in a grassy courtyard. The yards have fruit trees, low shrubs, and sometimes flowers. During the dry season the village looks sunbaked, while during the rainy season the corn is in various stages of growth, and the vista is green and luxuriant.

THE HOUSE AND COURTYARD

Ideally, a group of siblings, together with their wives and families, will occupy separate dwelling units surrounding a common courtyard. We designate this cluster of structures and accompanying courtyard by the term *compound*. Each nuclear family typically maintains separate sleeping and cooking facilities and eats apart from the others while it shares the courtyard and engages in a number of common activities with the other families. There are two distinct kinds of structures within a compound, even in those cases where it is occupied by only one family. These two structures are the cook shack and the main room used for sleeping, storage, and visiting. We shall refer to the main room as the house and understand that all cooking takes place in the cook shack located adjacent to or near the house.

The arrangement of the compound varies a great deal but almost always includes a house and cook shack for each family. The women, children, and older people spend most of their time within the compound, while the adult men are usually away at their fields during the day. Children play with and are cared for by their siblings and cousins within the compound, and the majority of their play activity, especially in the early years, is confined to the area.

The usual house in the barrio is rectangular, one room, windowless, and with only one door. It is made of adobe and usually has a tile roof. The adobe is made by members of the barrio and is available during all times of the year except during the rainy season. The houses have a gabled roof with heavy beams that are hand cut. These beams form the frame for the tiles that are placed from bottom to top to make the roof. These beams are brought from the mountain sides by burros and are later cut by hand. There are few hung doors, but doorways have a high wooden doorstep that one must step over and usually down into the house. Many have only boards for a doorway or a small fencelike partition that may be put up at night or when the family is out. The floor is dirt and is usually rough in some spots, particularly where there has been frequent walking and sweeping.

Horizontal beams along the top of the room form a space used for storage. There are no two-storied houses in the barrio. Houses, on the outside, are all adobe, unplastered, and unpainted. A few of the houses are plastered inside and painted white, with a strip of color around the bottom as a border.

For a very few families the cook shack is the only structure, but this is the rare exception rather than the rule. The cook shack is always made of sticks or of palm, not adobe, and generally has a thatched rather than tile roof. The hearth is sometimes in the center of the room but usually is back against a well-blackened corner. There are no ovens or other special construction for cooking, the only equipment consists of large rocks or broken pots turned upside down around a small fire to form support for the cooking pot or the flat *comal* for tortillas. Wood is usually used as fuel but little is kept inside the cook shack, most of it being stacked in the yard. There is a great deal of smoke in the cook shack when a fire is going, and if a child wants warmth or if the mother needs help, he must remain in this stuffy, smoky room, often with tears running down his face from smarting eyes.

Every house has an altar inside the main room, never in the cook shack. It is always up off the floor on boards, or planks on boxes, or perhaps on a table. Tables and chairs are made in the barrio by two carpenters and can be purchased fairly cheaply; so several families own them. Also, small woven chairs can be purchased very inexpensively from travelers from the mountains. Prints or colored pictures of the saints, some framed or some unframed, and perhaps even an image, will be found on the altar, but very seldom will a crucifix be seen. There will always be flowers of some sort in tin cans, sometimes fresh, more often faded or withered. Dried-up flowers seem to be as acceptable as fresh ones. There may even be some dusty paper ones. Candles are usually found on the table, but only the very small ones purchased at the store are upright. All the others lie flat on the table until the time comes to use them. They are very important in all ritual functions. There is always a container for the special Indian incense, *copal,* which also finds its way into all ritual activities.

Many other little items that might be pretty or interesting are found on the altar table, such as gourds, pretty stones that the wife might like, or some colored paper streamers. It often appears that the altar is merely a convenient place to dump all the odds and ends that sometimes come in handy and that the people do not want on the floor. The altar may become a very untidy spot in a room that is otherwise quite neat. It is customary for visitors to cross themselves in front of the altar on entering and leaving the house. This practice, however, is not rigidly adhered to except on such special occasions as fiestas.

The main room usually contains a chest or a trunk in which extra or fiesta clothes are kept. This chest is usually the bridal chest, presented to the girl at her wedding, although all sorts of family clothing are later kept in it. It may be very simple or ornately varnished, painted, or carved. However, it is usually kept up off the floor on planks or a trestle.

Corn on the ear is often stored in the main room and carried to the cook shack for shelling as needed. Granaries as such are very rare.

Most people sleep on the floor on palm mats that are made in the village and are very cheap. These are also used to sit on, and a woman grinding usually kneels on an old one or a piece of one. Every household, even the poorest, has several palm mats.

There may be a few chairs, generally small ones, close to the ground, much like a child's chair. The chairs are usually offered to guests as a form of respect, and almost every house has at least one or a substitute like a smooth log or small box to offer. When the man is in the house, he commonly sits on the chair or on the wall bench while the woman will sit on the mat on the floor. At all the fiestas this same pattern is carried out, the men sitting on the benches or the chairs around the walls of the room and the women sitting on the floor on mats. Perhaps if one sits on one's heels, as the men do, it is easier to sit on a chair or bench than if one sits on one's legs or with crossed legs as the women do. Perhaps an early habit of sitting controls the way in which furniture is later used. There is little other furniture in the house.

Most families do have a good collection of pottery or dishes, none of which is made in town but which is brought into market from the mountains by villagers who make them on the hillsides. Each house has several kinds, and some have many of the same type. There are usually the following: cups and bowls of various sizes, the clay *comal* for cooking tortillas, the lime pot, the pot for boiling corn, the bean pot, a large bowl for washing, and a water jar.

Water is brought to the home from the *barrancas*, the small tributaries of the river, or from wells. All of the people with wells tend to share the water with whomever asks, and some courtyards may have as many as six outside families entering once or twice a day for water. There is no monetary payment for this water, but flowers, a candle, or a choice bit of food may be carried to the wife on occasion.

No courtyard in the barrio has a bathroom or even a privy. People go to the fields or the river banks or to a particular corner of the courtyard, leaving the rest of the courtyard clean. The roads are also kept clean. Every householder is required to clean the street outside his house each day or whenever it is dirty, and in general the people of the barrio are careful, so that the streets are usually clean. The only dirty sections are those by vacant lots where there are no houses along the road. Almost all the yards and houses are kept very orderly with everything in its place.

In the courtyard outside the cook shack many pots can be seen drying on the ground in the sunshine. Inside the shack, implements and tools are hung on the walls or kept very neatly in one corner. The Indians seem to be careful not to have a great many things around for which there is not a definite use. They do not put things away and save them for the future. If they should come upon or be given an item for which they have no use, they either find a use for it or give it to someone else. There are not many things in the houses that do not receive frequent use.

COMMUNITY BUILDINGS

On one of the wider streets of the barrio is a corner store of the type found in el Centro, the only one that exists in the barrio. The non-Indian storekeeper (who is the barrio's only resident "outsider") sells primarily refreshments—soft drinks, candy, cigarettes, and locally made beer—and deals largely with people passing through the barrio on the way to el Centro. Barrio people buy candles, matches, aspirin, and mentholatum there, and children go there to spend a few centavos on sweets.

Farther down this same street, at the geographical center of the barrio, is the church, the religious center of the barrio. The fiestas, which are the major social and ceremonial events, are held in the church and its yard. It is in the barrio church that the images of Santo Domingo and Santiago, the patron saints of the barrio and of the town, respectively, are housed. It stands on a piece of open ground, one of the few plots in the barrio that is owned by the Indian population. Like the main church in el Centro, it is whitewashed adobe and very old. It is much smaller than the main church and is furnished inside with only a few movable benches instead of pews. (Most of the worshippers sit on the adobe floor or stand.) It has a high bell tower that is climbed by barrio men to ring the bell to announce a mass or a fiesta or a death in the barrio. The priest from el Centro comes to the church to hear confession on Saturday evenings, and early on Sunday morning (before mass in the main church) he says mass in the barrio. Weekly mass is attended mainly by women and children under 12. A nun and one or more young assistants come to the church from el Centro every

Thursday afternoon to give a class in catechism for children, and from 15 to 35 children under 12 attend more or less regularly. They gather before church to play in the churchyard, and they also meet there on the fringes of adult fiesta activities. Of particular interest to children are the preparations for fiestas—the construction of decorative arches and of fireworks displays—which take place in the church courtyard for several days before each fiesta.

The common civic center for the barrio is the *comunidad*. Because of the encroachment of townspeople on the land of the barrio, the comunidad is today separated from the barrio by town houses and fields at the northern edge. It consists of three large rooms surrounding a very large, bare courtyard. The more social, rather than religious, aspects of major barrio fiestas are set in the comunidad, as are the meetings of old men of the barrio to discuss matters of common interest. Children visit the comunidad during fiestas when their parents attend. They sometimes cross the yard on the way to school, but they are rarely to be seen there alone at any other time. (This fact may be related to the present location of the comunidad in el Centro, for barrio children tend to stay within the boundaries of the barrio for reasons we shall discuss below.)

BARRIO BOUNDARIES

At the southern edge of the barrio is the river. It is swift and narrow as it comes down from the hillside, but as the slope becomes less steep, the river widens and slows its pace. High on the hillside, some of the water is diverted into a canal that carries it through the streets of the barrio to irrigate fields in the valley. Lower down, the river is used for bathing and washing of clothes. Washing at the river is done about once a week, but bathing there is less frequent during the cold months. The river is enjoyed as a beautiful place, as well as a practical one, and adolescents use it as a setting for courtship. Young children may go with their older sisters while the latter wash clothes and flirt with boys. The river is forbidden to small children alone.

Beyond the river on the south and west are the fields owned and worked by barrio men. The farthest of them are as much as an hour and a half's walk away, and many others are half an hour away from the village. Men go to the fields when there is work there throughout the growing season, and when a boy is 12 years old, he goes and works beside his father. Younger boys do not go to work but many carry their fathers' midday meals to the field and stay to return with them at dusk.

Women and girls, as well, go to the fields at planting and at harvest; then the whole family lives in a temporary shelter for four or five days, eating and sleeping there until the work is finished. If there is a new baby in the family, the mother usually does not go on these expeditions, and small children are sometimes left behind with a grandmother or other relative.

Children must learn to walk long distances early. If the whole family goes to the field, all but the baby must walk the complete distance. A child does not ask to be carried but the father or an older sister may volunteer to carry a 2- or 3-year-old the last part of the way if he is lagging behind and detaining the family. The small children will also walk up the hillside 1 or 2 miles to the river each Sunday for bathing or washing of clothes.

The hills rise steeply on all sides of the barrio and its fields. Firewood is there for the taking, and families, including older children, make semiannual trips during the slack season to gather it. Herds of cattle, belonging to townspeople, and sheep, which some barrio members also own, graze on the hillsides. Few children play on the hillside unless they are watching a grazing herd. Early in the spring, children go with great enjoyment to collect flowers, which are used to decorate altars in the church and in homes. On these excursions an older sister or an adult is always present to supervise the younger children. The walk is exhausting for the youngest of them, and it is not surprising that they do not venture this far often.

There are few dangers in the barrio for children. There are almost no harmful snakes or animals in the natural environment and few poisonous insects. Only the oxen, which plod down the street during the work day, and the sheep and goats on their way to and from pasture must be avoided. All adults or older children warn younger ones to get out of the way when these animals approach and, if necessary, move them to safety.

For the typical barrio adult male the universe is spatially limited, and his horizon does not extend much beyond the valley he knows so well. This is not because he has never seen or visited other localities; most males have visited Oaxaca or Puebla at one time or another, and during the war some even got to the United States as unskilled laborers, although none stayed long enough to learn any English. These outside cities, so briefly visited, are part of the Indian's universe only in a most casual sense. Their local focus and main identifications center around the barrio itself. This localization of identification is even more striking for the women and children. None identify much with the larger town of Juxtlahuaca, let alone with the state. If outside the community and asked where they are from, they answer, "barrio Santo Domingo, Juxtlahuaca," or sometimes just, "the barrio," if the questioner is acquainted with the region.

The Indians regularly attend only three fiestas outside their own community—in Copala, Tecomastluahuaca, and Santa Rosa. Only adults and nursing infants in their mothers' arms go to Copala. Copala lies about eight hours south of Juxtlahuaca and has an annual fair and fiesta that draws people from a very wide area, including several adjacent districts. Indians from several different cultures and languages attend, and it is a great adventure for the barrio members. Copala is occupied by Trique Indians who speak a language very different from the Mixteco used in the barrio. In a real sense, Copala represents the southern boundary of the real social universe of the barrio, and though people know the names of villages, only a few men have ventured much farther south than Copala. (This statement does not apply to the townspeople, who have a much wider outlook and frequently trade great distances.) Santa Rosa is shown on the map, about 2 miles down the valley, and is only about 30 minutes' walk away. These people are very close to the barrio and are said to have moved from the barrio a few generations ago. Although the barrio, on the whole, tends to be endogamous, when people do go outside for marriage partners, they generally look to Santa Rosa. It is the only village, according to the barrio Indians, where Mixteco is spoken without an accent. The main fiesta in Santa Rosa, a religious event, is in August and is heavily attended by barrio residents. The annual fair in Tecomastlahuaca, on the other hand, is mainly a commercial affair, but many barrio members attend for the excitement of the large crowds it attracts. Children may go to affairs in both Santa Rosa and Tecomastlahuaca with their parents. Other than visiting in Santa Rosa with relatives, however, children very rarely go beyond Juxtlahuaca and the fields and hills immediately surrounding it. Under no circumstances would a boy or girl under 14 go as far as Santa Rosa without an escort.

Children rarely go even to el Centro without their parents or, if alone, without a legitimate errand, for el Centro is separated from the barrio not only geographically but by sociocultural barriers as well. Townspeople, in contrast to Indians, speak only Spanish and place a low value on Mixteco. They dress in Western-style, though rural, clothing, both men and women wearing shoes (although frequently without socks). The rebozo is worn by townswomen as well as by Indians, but in town it is brightly colored and is never draped in the Indian fashion. Coats also substitute for the rebozo in town. Women of el Centro often wear their hair loose, or curled by permanent wave, and many use make-up. Men of the town wear ready-made clothing of better quality than the average Indian's. Thus, even before he speaks, the barrio member is immediately recognizable as an Indian.

Indians are different from townspeople, and townspeople attach a negative value to this difference. They look down on the people of the barrio, and barrio people avoid interacting with them whenever possible. Townspeople and barrio members do meet at the market and in the stores of the town. (The food habits of the two groups are sufficiently different that such encounters are not as frequent as one might suppose. Indians consume no canned goods and buy very little meat, while town diet is varied.) At the market, interaction is limited to the specific act of buying and selling, and the Indian waits until all townspeople have been served. He is sometimes refused service altogether and is from time to time addressed or referred to in a derogatory way. The prices he pays and the prices he receives for his products are set by the townspeople.

Formally, the whole town is under the political leadership of an elected president. In fact, the barrio takes no part in the election of the president (or any other officials of the state or nation) and participates little, if at all, in the political affairs of the town. A representative of the barrio, the *regidor*, appointed by the president, has a certain amount of autonomy in barrio affairs. He is empowered to call for labor when the barrio streets or irrigation system or church need repairs, and all adult males in the barrio are required to serve their turn. He and his two assistants are also responsible for the selection and installation of the *mayordomos*, whose role as organizers of barrio fiestas we shall discuss later.

The barrio maintains its own church and celebrates its own annual series of fiestas. However, on a number of occasions throughout the year barrio people attend the main church. When they take part in processions originating in the town church, Indians walk at the end of the line. During the *Posadas* of the Christmas season, in which a procession ends in a private home, townspeople enter the house and Indians remain outside. When food is served, the townspeople are served first, the Indian men at the same table later, and the Indian women, on the floor in the kitchen, last of all.

Among adults, derogation of Indians by townspeople and deference to townspeople by Indians seem to be the accepted pattern of behavior. Among children, however, open aggression is not at all uncommon. Barrio children on their way to market or to school are in danger of attack, either verbal or physical (stone throwing), by town children. Since they are trained not to fight back, they are in real danger of being hurt. It is thought best by barrio parents for the child to remain in the barrio, which is his home, and not to go into the town, where he may come into conflict. Some give this reason for not sending their children to school.

The most important product of this social situation is an *esprit de corps,* a sense of solidarity among barrio Indians that is unknown in the town. Membership in the barrio community is highly valued by those inside it.

SOME BARRIO ATTITUDES ABOUT THE WORLD

Before going into detail about the cultural context of the child training practices, we would like to present a few reflections of the adult view of life and the universe. This should give the reader a quick preview of the general nature of the temperament of the people we will be talking about.

The basic assumption of the Indian man about the world in which he lives seems to be that it operates according to certain rules or laws ultimately controlled by that part of the universe which we would call the supernatural. He also believes that the general plan of things is ongoing and immutable and therefore that man must learn certain patterns of action and attitudes to bring himself into conformity with this scheme of things; that if he does so, he will receive the minimum amount of punishment and the maximum reward. There is the feeling that some suffering or misfortune is inevitable, but there are certain ways of avoiding it or mitigating it once it has fallen. In the Indian scheme of things in the barrio, the individual seems to be somewhat submerged in the group, that is, the individual exists as a member of a group that is adjusted to nature, and by following its pattern, he survives and prospers.

The barrio man recognizes change but does not project these changes into the future. He lives more or less in the timeless present, in which the known pattern is continued indefinitely. The barrio man identifies with the land, and there is a reciprocal relationship between the *milpa* (cornfield or cultivated place) and the man. The man's fulfillment, in one sense, comes from his opportunity to work out this adjustment between himself and his land, and it is interesting that he always works it with others. He seems to get the same pleasure from working with his friends in their fields as he does in his own fields. The Indian, as contrasted with the Spanish element in the town, sees the weariness that comes from physical toil as one of the facts of life, and he receives the approval of his fellows for working.

One might say that in his relation with other men in the barrio the Indian pattern is adjustive and permissive, while within the town the Spanish pattern is one of ordering and dominating. The statuses of leadership in the barrio, such as the *mayordomos* and *regidor,* are thought of as obligations rather than something to be striven for competitively. Every man from the barrio who follows the pathway of the culture and gains the respect of his fellows may expect to assume positions of prominence during his lifetime. However, these statuses are not thought of as a restrictive group of prizes for which many must compete and few attain. Envy and competitiveness are regarded as a minor crime. An Indian in a position of prominence never gives orders to his fellows. He may point out the pattern to be followed in a ritual or suggest practical modes of action, but this is in the manner of dispensing knowledge, not of dominating others either by force of personality or by authority of position. Age gives knowledge and wisdom and is respected as such.

Group decisions are made by consensus rather than by majority rule or dictatorial fiat. Perhaps it can be said that almost all the patterns of social activity in the barrio lead toward merging with the society rather than individual distinctiveness. The approved way of doing things is to live and let live and to adjust to other human beings to avoid conflict. This does not mean highly organized cooperation, although men do work together in groups that move from one field to another. However, each family has its own property, and each individual family goes about its business, not interfering with others although cooperating within a wide range of activities, such as planting and harvesting.

In the barrio, when a man takes a post of public responsibility, for example, as *mayordomo,* his wife shares the honor and responsibility. The man and woman in the barrio, as husband and wife, form a cooperative unit in the pattern of adjustment, and to this working team are added the children when they reach 8 or 10 years of age. Exploitation of one sex by the other is atypical, and children are not dominated primarily by physical or other heavy punishment. Bickering and fighting by teammates are not characteristic. Again, it seems that adjustment without friction is the goal, and, if this proves to be impossible, withdrawal rather than domination is the answer.

Overt interest in sex is fairly rare in the barrio; this is not to say that there is no interest in sex but rather that sex is regarded as necessary and natural. From the barrio point of view, the use of sex for exploitative purposes is inconsistent with their attitudes, just as are all other forms of exploitation of human beings. Sexual power does not add to the luster of the individual within the barrio.

Just as there seems to be no compartmentalization or stratification of the society among the Indians, similarly, there is no compartmentalization of the universe and supernatural matters. What we might call the supernatural is not clearly distinguished in the barrio; rather, the universe is seen as a more or less integrated whole. Among these nominally Catholic people there still persists a basic notion that the planting ceremonies, the rain-making ceremonies, and so on, operate without any distinction between empirical and spiritual world.

In the barrio, the personality of the typical individual—provided of course that his routine is not interfered with too much by the townspeople—is relatively more secure and better integrated than that of the townsperson. The Indian seems to follow the approved patterns of culture without any strong motivations toward special rewards, distinctions, prominence, or the like. This is evident, for example, in the work patterns of the Indians, in which they follow with the utmost diligence the standard routine, such as milpa work, corn grinding, and so forth. This same careful following of pattern is similarly followed in such ceremonial activities as the fiestas and the cofradia ceremonies. For a great many reasons, it seems that the Indian maintains a personal security so long as he stays within the framework of his culture and is able to follow the pathways without a great deal of deviation. However, we should say that the barrio person does not show an extreme of flat emotional reaction. The *abrazo* or semiritual embrace is given, for example, although not with a great show of enthusiasm. Joking is characteristic, but somewhat constrained. On the other hand, within the patterns of their life—and this is particularly noticeable in the fiesta pattern—a great deal of flexibility is allowed as long as the major outlines of the pattern are followed, so that though they appear somewhat compulsive, this is not carried to the extreme. They are not given to overexpression of emotions, though they can on occasion give vent to their emotions in an explicit way.

In the following chapters we shall outline the cultural context of child training practices, as well as the practices themselves, in an attempt to show how children are equipped to take their places in barrio life.

✹
✹
✹

Chapter 2

Daily Routine

The day begins in the barrio household between 5:30 and 6:00 A.M. The woman gets up from the mat on which she has slept, smooths her clothes, perhaps shakes her rebozo and throws it around her shoulders. She does not stop at this hour to wash her face or arrange her hair, for she must start the fire, heat the coffee (if there is any) for breakfast, and begin the preparations for the rest of the day's meals. Firewood is kept stacked in the courtyard, and she goes outside to select some pieces for the day. She lights the fire with a match, tends it until it is going well, and then puts a little pot of water into the coals to boil for coffee. If she plans to have her corn ground at the mill, she must go at once. When she returns, she takes the *masa* (coarsely ground corn) to the metate for its second grinding. If she is doing all of the grinding herself, she will have ground it through once instead of taking it to the mill. While she is grinding, her husband awakens and gets up. She may stop her grinding to serve him some coffee and a cold tortilla or two which have been stored since the preceding day. When he has eaten, he goes to his field if it is nearby and does not return until breakfast time at about 9 o'clock. Meanwhile the children awaken. A mother does not stop grinding corn to attend to the children as they get up. There is little dressing to be done, for children as well as adults sleep in all their clothing and need only shake out their rebozos or serapes and put them on again. The children often sit outside in the sunshine to get warm and wake up. Then they too eat a cold tortilla before beginning to play or to help their mother.

The woman is occupied with the making of tortillas until breakfast time. The children play in the courtyard or in the cook shack while she works, and she seldom notices them unless some difficulty reaches her ears. The oldest of the little girls is in charge of the younger children and watches them play. An older boy may take this opportunity to lead the burro or other animal to pasture, or he may split firewood in the yard. The family gathers at about 9 o'clock to eat the morning meal. The time for this meal, as for all others, is not set and may vary widely from day to day, but the content—cold beans, fresh tortillas, and chile—is always the same. The man and boys are served first, all sitting on the floor, the woman waiting on them and sometimes making tortillas as they eat them. After eating, the man goes outside and sits in the sun while the children are fed, and then he returns to the fields. When the younger children have returned to their play, the woman and older girl (if she has been helping with the meal) sit down to eat. After the meal, the woman washes the bowls in clear water and sets them aside. She washes the empty bean pot also and leaves it ready for the beans she will soon set on the fire for the midday meal.

During the morning the woman of the household may go to the market (if it is Friday) either to sell some garden produce or to buy food. On other days she might make purchases in a store. However, many small items of food are obtained by barter within the barrio, among friends, and this sort of exchange is carried on later in the day. When a woman goes to market, she may take her children with her. It may be necessary for them to sit with her quietly for several hours at a time. There is never any noise or interference from these children. They are simply there. Nursing infants, who might create a problem, are usually left behind, often with a woman friend or relative who can nurse the baby if the mother is delayed. A mother of a young infant might send her daughters or her younger sons to the market or the store rather than go herself. Adults and children alike tend to go about their errands with dispatch. Women, especially, do not stand in the street to gossip with friends. They greet neighbors in a friendly way but do not stop to converse. Even if a woman should meet her husband in the street, she does not talk with him at any length until they have reached home. In contrast, in the market place itself there is a great deal of conversation between women who sit next to each other hour after hour.

At home there are many tasks to be accomplished before noon. Preparations for dinner begin soon after breakfast is over. Beans are winnowed by pouring them from one hand to the other, then rinsed and placed in a pot of water on the fire. Corn is removed from the ear and boiled in lime water, then drained and ground. Children— girls of all ages and younger boys—may help with the preparation of beans and may carry corn from the storeroom and help to shell it. Only older girls grind corn. Water must be brought in for use in cooking and for drinking during the day. The source of water is usually a well at some distance from the house, for not all households have wells; those with water share it with their neighbors. The woman will often leave her children in the care of their older sister and go to get water herself, for this is considered heavy work. However, children of all ages, both boys and girls, can and do carry water. Poultry and pigs must be fed by the woman or the younger children. The house must be straightened up and the house and courtyard swept. The woman rarely does this herself unless she has no children, for girls and younger boys do the work under her supervision.

An older daughter may go once a week to the river to wash, a task which requires spending the whole day. For this reason, a mother with a nursing infant is not usually called on to do the laundry, nor is a woman who has full responsibility for the preparation of meals. If there is a relatively unoccupied woman or girl in the compound, she goes to do the washing. Otherwise mother and children go to the river together, and the children play while the mother washes and spreads the wet clothes on the grass and on bushes to dry in the sun.

For much of the average morning the woman is either away from home on an errand or, more frequently, bent over the fire and the metate in the cook shack. Children who sit in the kitchen near their mother may be asked to hand her a utensil from time to time, to bring a piece of firewood from the yard, to chase the chickens away from the corn, or to drive the dog from the doorway. They may munch a cold tortilla, a piece of fruit, or a handful of pumpkin seeds as they watch her work.

Children of school age may spend the morning and the afternoon at school, coming home for dinner between 1:30 and 3 o'clock. However, only about half of the barrio's school-age children go to school at all, and even those who do attend do so irregularly. Thus, when their morning chores are finished, many barrio children are free to play. Some children play alone, particularly those who live in nuclear households and have only infant siblings or siblings much older than they. More often, children play in courtyard groups that include their siblings and their cousins. While children in the courtyard are young, play groups may include both sexes under the direction of an older girl in the family who is entrusted with the care of the younger boys and girls. As soon as they are old enough to do without a caretaker, boys tend to play with other boys and girls who have no caretaking responsibilities tend to play with other girls. When boys and girls beyond the toddler stage play together, they usually play on the boys' terms.

The man of the household may or may not come home for dinner. If his field is within easy walking distance from the house, he may be at home for both breakfast and dinner. If it is farther away, he may wait until breakfast is over before he leaves, and in this case breakfast is served well before the usual 9 o'clock. He also stays in the field until late in the day, and his dinner is brought to him there by his wife or often by an older boy who is not yet old enough to work in the fields for a full day. The boy stays with his father after dinner and returns home with him at the end of the day.

If dinner is not yet ready when the man arrives, he may take a few minutes to play with his children or sit among the children while he chats with the friends or kinsmen who have come home from work with him. When dinner is ready, the man and boys are again served first; when they have finished, they may smoke a cigarette outside. The man generally does not return to the field after dinner, but neither does he spend the late afternoon at home alone. He gets together with other men in his compound or in another to visit or to do business. The talk centers around the crops, prices, and coming fiestas. He may spend the time making something—leather goods, adobes, tile —which he will later sell. He may gather materials to build a new house at some future time. He may work with other men on the decorations for a fiesta. Older boys may spin tops or shoot marbles with friends in the street. Later they may cut hay for the animals and bring the animals home to be fed.

Meanwhile the woman and girls clear the kitchen after dinner, putting aside the leftovers—beans, tortillas, and chile—once again for the evening meal. (Second helpings, at least for children, are discouraged, and food left over after a meal is saved rather than distributed.) Then the woman may visit a neighbor, usually going with some sort of excuse, for example, an exchange of food or a question about plans for a coming fiesta. When this small business has been taken care of, the women sit and visit at length. The guest may be offered coffee, fruit, or squash cooked in brown sugar, for "little gifts make for good friends." The women may comb and delouse each other's hair and that of the children who have come along on the visit. Corn may be shelled by all of the women present. Some of them may sew or embroider. The children play in the courtyard largely unnoticed.

Instead of visiting in the afternoon, a woman may engage in some money-making project at home, such as butchering a pig and rendering the lard for sale, toasting pumpkin seeds, gathering greens and herbs, or picking fruit. Such activties are often shared by other women in the compound.

At dusk water is carried from the well for evening use. The fire is built up and the tortillas reheated or, less frequently, made fresh. Supper—leftover beans and tortillas with chile—is the end of the day for the family, and after the dishes are put away and the corn set to soaking for the morning, the adults sit and talk around the smouldering fire. Candles and ocote are used sparingly, so the room is usually dark, except for firelight, long before bedtime. The children lie down and sleep when they are ready, and even the adults are usually asleep by 9 o'clock.

Special events require a number of alternative routines. On Thursday afternoons some children of school age go to catechism class at the barrio church. On Sundays some women arise earlier than usual in order to attend mass, but not all women go, and attendance is rather irregular at best. Children may or may not go with their mothers to mass. Also, on Sunday, many people go to the river to bathe. The whole family may go at once, but more often the women of a compound and all the children go together. The bath takes place soon after noon, during the warmest part of the day, and the hair is washed and clothing changed. There is much visiting and chattering in such a group. On Sunday afternoons some barrio men play softball on a field at the edge of the barrio using equipment that they own cooperatively. A few younger, generally single, barrio men spend Sundays drinking with their friends, and there may be a drunk or two in the streets of the barrio on Sunday evening. These are the exception rather than the rule, except on fiesta occasions.

During the week the man of the household may, instead of going to the field, engage in some special semiskilled work. He may make or lay adobe or tile or do carpentry on contract, and while he is working, he may receive a midday meal from his employer. This is particularly true if he is working for another barrio person. On other days he may take part in a cooperative work group in the field of a friend, and on these days, he eats a festive meal with the group. During the dry season he may be called on to help on the same basis in the construction of a friend's house. The woman of the household that has requested cooperative help prepares the meal for the workers with the aid of her daughters and other women in her compound.

A man's labor may also be required by the regidor. The *tequio*, or communal work, includes planting and tending corn in the communal fields, street cleaning, repairs or improvements on the church, and so on. The church bell rings to announce the time, but the 30 men needed on any given day are notified in person beforehand. Records are kept by the regidor of each man's participation. The *tequio* is seldom accompanied by a communal meal.

Fiestas of all kinds alter the daily routine, even when the household is not directly involved in them, for the gift of food from someone else's fiesta makes it unnecessary for the woman to prepare a meal for the family. Besides providing good fare fiestas offer an opportunity for visiting and drinking. Barrio saints' fiestas also entail entertainment—dances, dramas, fireworks displays, and the movement of crowds. They include special masses which are attended by the majority of barrio residents. When the man of the household is a member of the society that is responsible for the fiesta, the routine is even more strikingly changed. For several weeks preceding the fiesta, especially if it is an important one, much of the man's time and energy goes into preparations for the event. He takes part in the purchase of food, liquor, cigarettes, and ritual necessities, such as candles. He participates in the gathering and arrangement of materials used in decoration of the church and adornment of the saint. He may help to build a structure on which fireworks are to be displayed. He spends much time in meetings with the other members of the society, planning and collecting money. On the days of the fiesta itself (which may last from two or three days to as long as two weeks), he rises early, attends mass, and then gathers with the other men of the society for a breakfast served by all of their wives. After breakfast they drink and smoke and make speeches until dinner. Between dinner and evening they drink again and watch the ceremonies that mark the particular fiesta. After dinner there are fireworks, a drama, or, often, a dance in which everyone participates until very late. Children sit and watch the dancing until they can stay awake no longer. Then they often go to sleep on the floor or in the arms of their mothers or sisters.

The woman whose husband is deeply involved in a fiesta is responsible for helping to prepare the food. Under the direction of the *mayordoma*, the wife of the head of the society, she works with other women (at grinding and tortilla making and the cooking of meat) from early morning until late, sometimes even sleeping in the fiesta cook house. The work is hard, but the interaction with other women is pleasant, and fiestas are anticipated with much excitement. Children may go with their mothers to the fiesta site, and here, as in the market, they sit and watch without interrupting. The youngest may be tied onto the mother's back while she works. Sometimes younger children are left at home with an older sibling; in this case, the woman leaves the fiesta at about 10 in the morning and again at 4 in the afternoon to take some of the fiesta food home to her children. Sometimes a woman arranges to do part of her work at home, for example, grinding and making a batch of tortillas. Then she sends her daughter with the finished tortillas to the fiesta place, and her share of the food is sent home to her. On fiesta days, meals are irregular, but children wait without complaint until their mother returns, and they enjoy the special meal when it is ready.

In general, barrio men spend very little time with their families. They are at home only briefly during the day, and even then their attention is often absorbed by business and the society of other men. Men are sometimes affectionate and playful with their children (especially the youngest) and often show pride in them before visitors. They are occasionally asked by their wives to discipline unruly sons. However, the only children who interact at all intensively with their fathers are boys of 12 years and over. Boys of this age work in the fields every day and begin to participate with the other men of the compound.

Similarly, barrio women are occupied almost full time with their primary responsibility—the provision and preparation of food for the family. When they are not busy in the kitchen, they are relaxing—always with hands at work—with other women in their own courtyard or a neighboring one, or they are chatting with others while selling fruits in the market. The youngest child and the oldest daughter receive more attention from their mother than any of her other children. A nursing infant must be attended to by his own mother whenever she is present, and, in addition to routine care, he receives many expressions of love, both verbal and physical. The oldest daughter, on the other hand, needs little care but much instruction. The mother teaches her to fulfill the feminine role by example, often calling her from play to watch some operation in order that she may learn to perform it. As the oldest daughter learns more and more of the appropriate role behaviors, she comes to interact with her mother and the other women of the compound as a woman among women.

Neither men nor women are often found playing with children. Thus children between infancy and young adulthood spend their days apart from adults for the most part. However, their play is often imitative of adult role behavior. They are content to watch adults at work and to be near them without doing anything else. They are happy, especially when very young, to perform little tasks for the adults around them. The daily routine in the barrio belongs to adults, and children observe it and practice it, first playfully and later in earnest, until they too are grown.

✤
✤
✤

Chapter 3

Economy and Diet

All the men in the barrio, save one, earn their primary living through
the cultivation of maize. Since most of the land in the valley belongs
to townspeople, barrio men farm land on the hillsides for the most
part. A few families own irrigated valley land near their houses and
plant corn there. Many are tenant farmers; they plant the plots adjacent to their houses and split the crop with the landowner who lives
in town. In addition, all men in the barrio may work land that is
communally owned by the barrio, and the produce of this land belongs
to them as usufruct owners. The communal land is in the hills, and
a fee of 50 centavos per *maquila* (approximately 4 pounds of seed)
planted is paid into the communal treasury for the use of the land. All
barrio men also contribute labor toward a collective harvest of corn on
part of the communal land, the sale of which benefits the barrio
treasury.

Corn may be planted four times each year, depending on the type
of land and the availability of irrigation. The first planting, which
depends solely on irrigation, is about the first week in February and
is called "early seed." It is harvested in late June and early July. The
second planting, called "half irrigation," takes place between the first
and the tenth of March. It is irrigated twice, and the rest of the moisture comes from the rain. Corn planted at this time is harvested from
the twentieth of July through early August. The third planting depends entirely on rain, taking place between March 20th and April 1st
(by which time some rain may be expected). It is called "cloud seed."
Harvesting of this crop takes place in late September and the first days
of October. The fourth planting, called "rain seed," takes advantage
of the *temporal*, the heaviest part of the rainy season. Seed is sown
from April 25th (the day of San Marcos) through the first few days of
May, and the harvest is reaped in mid-October. Planting high in the

mountains takes place in late February and March and harvesting in late November and on into January, depending on the time of planting.

The first step in preparing the land is the *barbecho* or breaking of the land. This is done with a crude wooden plow tipped with metal, pulled by a yoke of oxen that the owner of the field may own, borrow, or rent. After the plowing, the field is left for a month; then a second plowing, again using oxen, takes place. This plowing is called the *revuelta* or "turning over," and its purpose is to break the earth into smaller pieces and keep it from drying out. The field is left for another three months after the *revuelta*. Then, again with the plow and oxen, furrows are made in the soil. Within a month, the first rain comes and the field is planted. A hole is made with a *coa* or digging stick, a little water is poured into it by hand, and four to six seeds are dropped in. If beans or squash are being planted also, the seed of these are placed in the same hole. The hole is covered, and the sower moves on to the next spot about a meter away.

When the corn in the field, or *milpa*, is about a foot high (in about a month) the first weeding (*limpia*) takes place. The ground is turned over with a plow. A second limpia is performed in three weeks to a month, depending on the amount of rain. A third limpia is done by hand or with a hoe and consists of pulling out the weeds that have grown up close to the corn stalk and of heaping up the earth in hills around the base of each corn plant. The weeds pulled are used to feed livestock and may be brought in little by little instead of being harvested and stored all at once. When the corn has dried on the ear, the *pisca*, or harvest, takes place, the corn being removed from the stalks and carried unshucked to storage areas in the owner's house. The land is immediately prepared for another planting if it is flat and not stony. Hillside land and land full of stones are allowed to lie fallow for one or two years between plantings. High in the mountains, the fallow period is as long as four years.

If the field is irrigated, irrigation takes place for the first time ten days before the barbecho; next, a month after planting, twice more a month between the second and third limpias, and perhaps a fifth time if the soil is sandy. The irrigated field is left fallow until the following January when it is irrigated again, and the cycle repeats. The use of water for irrigation is regulated by the town government through the regidor and is subject to a fee.

Both planting and harvest are attended by the entire family, and usually four to six men in addition to the owner of the field help with the work and receive food and reciprocal help in their own fields in return. This system of cooperation holds true only within the barrio, for when a barrio man works for a townsperson, he is paid by the day and receives no meals. On the day of planting, the owner or some other member of the family (even one of the women) walks slowly around the field sprinkling aguardiente (a distilled sugar-cane liquor used in all ceremonial contexts) on the ground. Incense is burned and a candle lighted, and over these, prayers are said to the "owner of the earth" asking him for a crop this year as in other years. The aguardiente is interpreted as the first drink the earth receives—a kind of nourishment given to the "owner of the earth" in the hope of nourishment, in the form of a good crop, in return. Rarely now, but formerly often, the head of a turkey, chicken, or sheep was planted in the center of the field and stood for the earth's first food. After the earth has been offered drink, the people drink also and the planting begins.

Similarly, at harvest time, aguardiente is sprinkled on the ground before the assembled men begin to remove the ears from the stalks. When the corn is finally heaped up in the owner's storehouse, a candle is lighted and incense burned, and the family gathers around the mound to pray, giving thanks for a good harvest and asking that the corn last for a long time. When a stalk with three ears on it is found, it is brought back to the house intact and placed upright in the center of the mound of ears in order that the rest of the corn remain plentiful throughout the year.

Prayer is thought advisable, for farming is always hazardous, and many barrio families operate on a very narrow margin. Although irrigated land is twice as productive as *temporal* (yielding 120 *maquilas* per maquila sown, in contrast to about 60), it is scarce because of the physical limitations of the valley and the fact that it is owned primarily by the townspeople. As a result, it is expensive, and few barrio men can afford to plant enough of it to ensure a surplus. Many families cannot plant enough corn to meet their needs throughout the year. A few, who have become wealthy by barrio standards in ways we shall discuss below, have enough surplus to sell to merchants in el Centro and to outsiders who come to market. The average family grows enough corn to feed the household and the livestock and to pay for the bare necessities in the way of clothing. Food items that are not home-grown, of which some are staples, and extraordinary needs such as medical care, life-cycle ceremonies, and contributions to barrio fiestas must usually be financed in other ways.

OTHER SOURCES OF INCOME

Livestock is one supplement to family income, although it requires initial capital and is therefore differentially distributed among the households, depending on their wealth. Every household has some poultry—turkeys or chickens—for it is relatively inexpensive to feed and is an essential part of most household and community ceremonies. No one can afford to be without a chicken or turkey in case of an emergency. Chickens provide eggs that can be sold in the market or traded in the stores. Eggs are not eaten, as a rule, because they bring such a good price. Many families have pigs which may be sold or slaughtered, primarily for lard. Pork is part of one important ceremonial dish prepared for the patron saint's fiesta in July.

Most families have a burro or two, rarely more. These animals are useful for transporting corn from field to storehouse or market and for carrying wood from the hills. A few families have sheep or goats in small numbers. Very few have cattle, and horses are even more uncommon. Some of the barrio's cows are milked and the milk sold, largely in el Centro. Several men have teams of oxen which other men sometimes pay to use. Responsibility for the care of livestock is fairly clearly defined, women and young children attending to the pigs and poultry and boys (and, less often, men) to the burros and other large animals.

Alfalfa is grown by about ten barrio men and used to feed their own animals and to sell to others. Alfalfa must be irrigated once after planting, and during the year of its growth cycle, it can be cut five times. Since it requires even more hand labor than corn, the help of other men is always requested, and the first cutting is divided among them. The owner of the field receives all of the rest of the harvest.

Wage work within the barrio is unknown, but barrio men sometimes do farm work for townspeople, even though wages are extremely low. Better pay can be earned in Tlaxiaco, in the mines, or in the sugar refinery at Atencingo, Puebla. Several men, or occasionally a whole family, will go there to live and work for a period of weeks or months.

Half a dozen men have been as far as the United States as *braceros* for six months or more, and the wages accumulated during these periods have made one or two of these men rich by barrio standards. The land on which the barrio's wealthiest man plants some 35 *maquilas* of corn a year was bought with his American earnings.

Several men have part-time specialties which provide them with additional income. One man carves the wooden masks worn during the religious drama performed at the fiesta of the patron saint. Another bakes the bread served during this fiesta, a task which takes three to five days, and is reimbursed in food (enough for his family as well as himself). Several men serve as butchers at the fiesta and are paid in food. One man with grown sons still at home leaves them in charge of the milpa and makes regular trips to Copala to sell corn which he has bought for this purpose. The young men of another family work as carpenters in el Centro. Several others make or lay adobe or tile which they sell in the barrio and in town.

Many other small money-making projects are engaged in by women. Indeed, while only a few men have part-time specialties, nearly all women earn money in one or more ways. A great number of women make tortillas for sale. A woman who is fully involved in this activity will grind and prepare tortillas three times a day and will either take them to market or send a little girl to sit and sell them there or to deliver them by prearrangement to houses. Many other women sell products of their gardens—fruit, tomatoes, chiles—in season, or send their daughters to do so. A few women are well-known as expert embroiderers and sell blouse decorations to others. One or two have sewing machines and make clothing to order for other barrio people. (The one man who is not a farmer also has a sewing machine and does tailoring for men.) Women with no other means of support, widows primarily, gather firewood in the mountains, sell it to buy corn, and then make tortillas for sale to meet their daily needs. One barrio woman bakes bread, and several others prepare chocolate on order.

Among women, only young girls work for wages outside the barrio. Some of them work for families in el Centro, but wages there are less than half the daily rate for men, work is hard and demeaning for the most part, and fringe benefits are few. Many of the girls who are servants work as far away as Oaxaca and Mexico City for months at a time.

FOOD

Corn and beans are the basis of the barrio diet, and everyone in the barrio eats them daily from the time he is a few months old. Beans occur in wide variety. Of the five colors, the black, brown, and red are all grown in the barrio; spotted ones seem to grow wild and are brought in by mountain people on market day, and white beans grow at some distance away and are brought in by merchants. Beans are prepared by simmering them in a clay pot for many hours and are served with salt as the only seasoning.

Corn of four colors is grown in the barrio. The white is considered the best and may be used in all of the dishes made with corn. The yellow is in second place and is used mostly for tortillas. The red and the blue-black are harvested early and do not keep very well. These latter are eaten boiled, on the cob, having been picked before they have dried. The white and the yellow varieties are rarely served in this way.

Of all the ways of preparing corn, the tortilla is by far the most common. These thin, unleavened cakes are served with every meal and take the place of tableware, for people use them to carry food from the plate to the mouth. In the preparation of tortillas, the maize is first soaked overnight in lime water to soften the hulls and then ground on a *metate*. Many women nowadays take the boiled corn to one of two motor-driven mills located in el Centro on the edge of the barrio, although not all feel they can afford this luxury. Each morning quite early a line forms outside the mill, and women chat while they wait their turn. Since grinding corn is a woman's job exclusively, one of the mills is even run by a woman. Little boys do not go to the mill alone; and if they go with their mothers, they stay outside while the grinding is done.

Tortillas may be cooked twice, and this operation transforms them into *totopo*, a crisp, flat cake that can be carried on journeys for two or three days without spoiling. Maize is also prepared as *atole*, a gruel made of very finely ground corn with milk and water. For this purpose, milk, rarely used in any other form, may be bought by the cup from a passing vendor. Atole is the first solid food given to the nursing infant and is also served to invalids and the aged. Corn is also prepared as tamales, which are balls of corn dough enclosing meat or beans, wrapped in corn husk or palm leaves, and boiled. Still another way of preparing corn is *posole*, a festive dish, much like hominy grits, made with meat.

A great variety of chiles is used in cooking; and chiles, either whole or ground with tomato, are served with each meal of beans and tortillas. A sauce used with meat on festive occasions is made almost entirely of chiles of different kinds, ground to a fine paste on the metate, and cooked. Townspeople consider the Indians' use of chile excessive and have great difficulty in eating barrio ceremonial food for this reason. Only a small amount of chile is grown in the barrio, despite its importance in the diet, since climate limits its cultivation. Most of the chile consumed in the barrio is bought in the market from merchants from the coast. Salt, the only other seasoning in daily use, is also brought in from the coast or from the north and purchased at the market. Garlic, onions, pepper, cinnamon, and cloves, used in festive cooking, are purchased as needed. Other herbs which are used in preparing meat are gathered in and around the barrio, where they grow wild.

Meat in the form of chicken, turkey, beef, or pork is a luxury food and is consumed only at fiestas. However, various sorts of fiestas arise very frequently, on the average of once a week throughout the year, and therefore meat is not as minor an item in the diet as might be supposed. All kinds of meat are boiled, and various herbs are used as seasoning. Meat may be served in broth or in a chile sauce. It is held in a tortilla and eaten with the fingers.

Several kinds of fruit grow in the barrio. Pomegranates, bananas, avocados, and papaya are used at home and bartered or sold to other households. In addition, pineapples are occasionally bought in the market. Fruit is eaten casually, between meals, and is enjoyed by adults and children alike.

Squash may be cooked as a vegetable, with chile and herbs, or as a sweet, with brown sugar. In the latter form it is often eaten between meals, especially by children. The seeds of the squash are dried and toasted and served as another type of between-meal snack. Tomatoes are used primarily as a sauce with chiles added. Greens of various kinds, mostly gathered in the hills, are sometimes served boiled with a meal, but they are not an important part of the diet.

Coffee is drunk on arising by those families who can afford it. Coffee beans are bought from merchants from Copala and other coffee towns to the south. The bean is toasted on the comal, shelled by hand, and then ground on the metate. Coffee is made by boiling the coffee powder with a lump of dark, unrefined cane sugar.

Chocolate and bread are almost exclusively festive foods. The cacao bean is toasted, shelled, and ground like coffee. Next, however, the paste is ground again with white sugar and stick cinnamon and patted into small, round tablets. These tablets are dissolved in hot water to make the chocolate. Some women seem to be particularly able chocolate grinders, and they are sometimes hired to grind large quantities of chocolate for a fiesta. Chocolate is often served with bread as an early morning festive meal. The bread may be bought in the barrio, where one woman makes it regularly, or in el Centro stores. It is made into rolls, some white and some sugar-frosted. Once a year a special kind of bread, ordinary in shape but different in the proportion of shortening and in the use of eggs, is baked by a barrio man and assistants to be served at morning meals during the patron saint's fiesta.

Candy is eaten occasionally, for this is usually what a child buys with any money he may be given as a reward for obedience. It is available in the barrio's one store and in the stores of el Centro. Cigarettes are smoked by men on ceremonial occasions, rarely at other times. They may be bought at the store or rolled by hand from local tobacco. Wild tobacco is also chewed "to give one strength for one's daily work."

Aguardiente, a strong liquor made from distilled sugar-cane products, is drunk on all ceremonial occasions, often in great quantity. Men drink much more than women and are sometimes taken home at the end of an affair by their sober wives or by their children. On certain occasions, depending apparently on the supply of liquor or the inclination of the hosts rather than on the type of ceremony, women are vigorously encouraged to drink. However, only one woman in the barrio has been seen drunk, and she is the subject of much amused comment in the community. Beer is also drunk by some barrio men, although its use is infrequent partly because of its greater cost. It tends to be confined to ceremonies in which townspeople take part, for the people of el Centro deplore the barrio's enjoyment of aguardiente and often refuse to drink it.

The food and drink used daily are purchased in very small quantities, for there is never much money on hand in the average barrio household. Raising the cash for a major expenditure—a fiesta, for example—usually demands a major money-making effort. Corn or alfalfa or an animal must be sold or some family member must work for wages for a time. In an emergency, money may be borrowed, often from a kinsman or *compadre*. Wealthy townspeople are sometimes approached for a loan, but this is infrequent because the interest rate is about 10%.

CEREMONIAL REQUIREMENTS

The fiestas celebrated by the individual household on the occasion of the marriage, birth, or death of one of its members are partially supported by contributions of a few pesos from each family that attends. Nevertheless, much of the cost of the food—which may be served or distributed to the whole barrio—cigarettes and liquor, the incense and candles, the fireworks and the services of the priest must be borne by the family. The families of a bride and groom exchange sets of clothing for the couple. The family of the deceased provides the coffin. The *padrino* of the principal in any ceremony may help pay for liquor, cigarettes, decorations, and so on, and a baptismal *padrino* is especially likely to contribute clothing for the child, but all such contributions are voluntary. The less formal meals which are served to those who help with planting and harvest are always somewhat festive. Meat and aguardiente are essential. Contributions of money or liquor by the participants on such occasions are less frequent.

In addition to the above fiestas, which involve even poor families in the expenditure of money for ritual purposes, there are many fiestas of great community significance which are financed largely by those who can best afford it. Each of the major barrio saints has a *mayordomia*, a group of men who share the cost of the fiesta for the particular saint in a given year. The *mayordomo* bears the greatest financial burden, but his *diputados* share it, and contributions from invited guests may be expected. The expense involved in these ceremonies varies greatly, the mayordomo for the patron saint's fiesta being expected to put on the biggest show. Men are selected for these offices largely on the basis of their economic capability.

In comparison to any of these ritual requirements, the cost of curing illness is usually relatively minor. A great number of common ailments can be treated by the family itself with herbs or rituals which cost nothing. For more serious conditions a *curandero* or *brujo* may be summoned from the barrio or from a neighboring community. Midwives are employed to assist at a birth. Only rarely do barrio people consult the doctor in el Centro. However, such medicines as aspirin and mentholatum are rather widely used. They are bought in town stores at little cost.

OTHER NECESSITIES OF LIFE

Clothing is bought to wear for the first time at the fiesta of the patron saint in July. (However, not every member of the family has new clothes every year.) Some clothing is bought ready-made—the shirts and pants of men, huaraches, sombreros, rebozos, and serapes are sold in local stores. Hats are manufactured outside Juxtlahuaca and are imported in great numbers. Just before the big fiesta, they are sold at higher prices than during the rest of the year. All other clothing is made at home from yard goods bought in el Centro. The sewing may be done by hand, especially on blouses and on men's traditional clothing, but is often taken to a barrio seamstress who does it on her machine for a fee. The tailor mentioned previously makes Western-style shirts and pants for men.

Most adults have two sets of clothing, one to wear and one to wash. The very poor sometimes have less than this amount of clothing, but the rich seldom have much more. Extra cash tends to be invested in the family business in the form of land or animals or to be spent in community ceremonies. Little is used for personal adornment and relatively little for enrichment of the diet. Children, even of middle-income families, may have only one set of clothing and must either wrap themselves in a rebozo or blanket while it is laundered and dried or wear it dirty. Two children who attend the Catholic school wear school uniforms provided by their respective el Centro godparents. The barrio children who are in public school have no special school clothes. Worn clothing, especially men's work clothing, is mended and remended.

All household utensils, furnishings, and tools are purchased, and none of these are made anywhere in the barrio. Included are such items as pottery, baskets, metate, mano, rope, and mats. Chairs and wooden chests are made by el Centro carpenters. Metal tools—knives, machetes, hoes, coa and plow points—come from Oaxaca and are bought in el Centro stores. Even the less durable of these utensils— the pottery, baskets, and mats—need to be bought only infrequently, while the wooden and metal objects and the mano and metate may be bought only once or twice in a lifetime.

Resin-soaked pine, which is burned for light, may be cut in the mountains or purchased from the Indians of neighboring hamlets. A few families use kerosene lamps.

The nonfood items required for ritual are also largely purchased. The candles in common use are made in el Centro, although the mayordomia of the patron saint makes pure beeswax candles once a year for use in the church. The incense, copal, is a pine resin which can be gathered in the mountains but is often bought in the market from people who live in the mountains. The pictures of saints used on household altars are bought in el Centro stores. Although the decorations used in the church during fiestas are partly of store-bought crepe paper and cotton cloth, flowers and greens which grow in the area are an important material in adornment.

It is clear that the barrio household, only partially self-sufficient with regard to food and medicine, is even more dependent on the people of el Centro as manufacturers or middlemen for most of the other necessities of life. Housing can theoretically be obtained without spending much money, for most of the materials of a thatched adobe hut are free for the taking, and cooperative labor is used for the construction. Adobe is made of local clay and straw by the owner himself or by another barrio member (whom he pays). Roof beams and supports may be cut in the mountains. Doorsills and the infrequent doors are made locally, and thatching materials for cook shacks are gathered in the surrounding hills.

Tile for the roof of the main house must be bought in el Centro and laid by an artisan who charges for his services. A new house is therefore a major undertaking, and only the wealthy can build one

simply for the sake of greater comfort. A house may last for generations, and many a barrio member is born and dies in the same one
and passes it on to his children. A young married couple may live
with the husband's parents, in which case another fireplace in the cook
shack and perhaps another room on the main house are added. The
couple will, sooner or later, build their own separate house.

PROPERTY OWNERSHIP AND INHERITANCE

Everyone owns his clothing, and whatever he has worn (except
his blanket) is buried with him when he dies. All other possessions—
the utensils of the woman, the tools of the man, the land, the animals,
and the family house—are divided among the immediate family after
the individual's death. If a man has not made arrangements for his
inheritance in advance, his widow is in charge of the distribution of
property among their children. (A man's own siblings will not inherit
from him unless he has no children.) Both men and women may inherit, although a daughter will expect to receive less than her brothers.
Land and animals may be divided equally among the children, or
the eldest son may be given more than the others and be placed in
authority over his younger brothers and sisters, especially if they are
much younger. The house is usually kept by the widow until she re-
marries. Then it may be sold by the children and the money divided
among them or it may be bought by one of them from the rest, who
are then expected to leave it. In any of these situations, disputes may
arise among siblings. A widow may attempt to forestall an argument
by having the town judge preside over the distribution.

OVERVIEW

The subsistence of each barrio household is based, essentially, on
one crop. Cooperative arrangements and participation of the whole
household easily handle the labor problem. However, land availability
limits the production of corn to the extent that it is often difficult to
feed the family, much less to buy the many food items which supplement corn in the diet and the even more numerous items of clothing
and household equipment. Very few of the necessities of life are made
at home or obtained free. Opportunities within the community to
supplement the family income are limited and relatively little ex-
ploited—industry is nonexistent and animal husbandry is of little

economic importance. It is difficult to make ends meet in the barrio, and it is virtually impossible to become rich.

One can either remain poor, then, or leave the community in search of wealth. Many barrio people have chosen the latter alternative. However, leaving the community need not be permanent. Once having become relatively wealthy, it is possible to stay wealthy on one's return home. By investing his savings in land in the barrio, a returned laborer can produce a surplus of corn which allows him to reinvest in land, animals, and so forth, and thus to increase his income steadily through the years. Short of this, it is possible to improve one's financial condition in a more limited way by working long enough to pay for a new house or to pay off a debt. In either case, there is a commitment to permanent residence in the barrio on the part of most of those who leave it. Young girls come back before they are too old to marry, and men come back in time to accept a mayordomia. Most people seem to prefer to live in the barrio, more or less accepting its standard of living, rather than to seek a higher standard of living by leaving it permanently for the outside world. While the fact that money goes farther in the barrio than outside is certainly relevant, there is clearly more than economics behind their choice. The experience of barrio people with non-Indians has given them no reason to expect a warm welcome in the outside world.

Since human warmth matters to them, being a member of the barrio community is important in itself, and people are willing to spend money to increase their acceptability as members. A man may go away to work primarily in order to pay the expenses of a mayordomia, and the rest of the community notices and is gratified (or not) by the amount that he spends on food, liquor, and entertainment. Ceremonial spending, even at the household level, is subject to community comment. When the death of a rich man is announced, it is sometimes said that "a bull has died," meaning that a bull rather than a cow will be killed for the funeral feast. Tradition and opinion demand that those who have wealth share it, to some degree, with the rest. Respect and honor are the rewards for this kind of service to the community. On the other hand, display of wealth in personal adornment or consumption of alien foods is likely to be widely criticized. The economics of this situation can perhaps best be summarized in the words of Eric Wolf (1957) who describes the closed corporate peasant community (of which Juxtlahuaca's barrio is an example) in the following terms.

> Closed, corporate peasant communities . . . maintain a body of rights to possessions, such as land . . . (they) put pressures on members to redistribute surpluses at their command, preferably in the operation of a religious system,

and induce them to content themselves with the rewards of "shared poverty"
. . . They strive to prevent outsiders from becoming members of the community, and (place) limits on the ability of members to communicate with the
larger society. . . . (Their) internal function . . . is to equalize the life
chances and life risks of (their) members.

Closed corporate peasant communities . . . will strive to force co-members
to redistribute or destroy any pool of accumulated wealth which could poten-
tially be used to alter the land tenure balance in favor of a few individual
families or individuals. Purchase of goods produced outside the peasant sector
of society and their ostentatious display also rank as major social threats,
since they are prima facie evidence of an unwillingness to continue to redistribute and destroy such accumulated surplus. They are indications of an
unwillingness to share the life risks of fellow villagers according to traditional
cultural patterns. Among most peasant groups, as indeed among most social
groups anywhere, social relations represent a sort of long-term life insurance.
The extension of goods and services at any given moment is expected to yield
results in the future, in the form of help in the case of threat.

People of the barrio, then, generally feel the need of the life insurance their community can provide and are willing to pay for it in
terms of continued residence in the community and distribution of
surpluses according to traditional rules.

❋

❋

❋

Chapter 4

Family Organization and Kinship

THE EXTENDED FAMILY

The typical family in Santo Domingo is an extended one. While a
nuclear family, which characterizes our own society, consists of a husband and wife, together with their children, an extended family may
include married brothers, together with their wives and children. As
we shall see below, the families in Juxtlahuaca most frequently contain
two or three nuclear families within the same household.

These extended families are housed together within a jointly owned
compound which consists of a large area that generally has several

rooms and cook shacks around a common patio area. A compound has its limits defined by an adobe wall or, less usually, by a wire or wooden fence. Within the compound, each of the individual rooms is thought of as belonging to one or another of the family members. The patio area, however, is the common property, so far as use is concerned, of the whole family. The compound area will also include two or three cook shacks in which the adult women prepare food, as well as sheds for the burros and chickens and pigs.

Residence is ideally patrilocal, that is, at marriage the wife would move to reside with her husband, and the new couple would reside with or near the husband's father. When interviewed, people of the barrio say that such patrilocal residence is to be preferred. In actual practice there is a great deal of variation in residence patterns. A number of circumstances make it desirable for the husband to join his wife and live with or adjacent to her family. The major determinant as to whether or not a newly married couple will reside near the husband's family is the availability of space in the prospective compound, together with the relative economic position of the family. When the husband comes from a lower economic group, and his compound is already crowded, the couple may elect to live with the wife's family if there is room in that compound. In the event that there is no room in either of the compounds, the couple will tend to reside as closely as possible to one or the other set of parents; so, although they are not living in the same compound, they are very close, and the day to day interaction amounts to virtual membership in the extended family. Thus, for example, related children living in adjacent households frequently play together and interact very closely with each other regardless of the fact that they do not all share a single patio area and common compound.

The question arises as to whether to count adjacent families who are related and interact frequently as nuclear or extended. We have checked on the total barrio, counting them first one way and then the other. If we count them as nuclear families, we find that one third of the families in the barrio would be classed as nuclear families. On the other hand, if we count on the basis of interaction, relationship, and adjacency, then over four fifths of the families in the barrio live in extended families. For purposes of socialization, we feel that the second criteria is a better one to follow. On this basis, only 3 of the 22 intensively studied families would be counted as nuclear families.

The same distinction also affects the extent to which the ideal patterns of patrilocality are carried out. The ideally stated pattern of preference for patrilocal residence is not borne out by an actual statis-

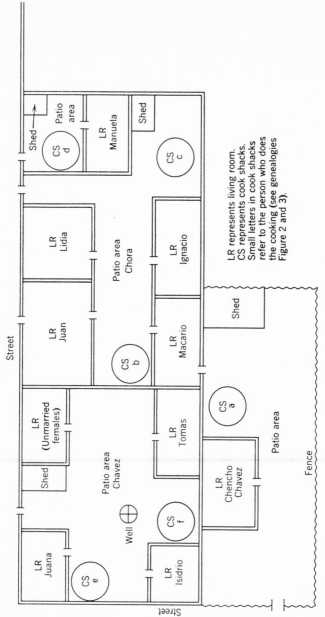

LR represents living room.
CS represents cook shacks.
Small letters in cook shacks
refer to the person who does
the cooking (see genealogies
Figure 2 and 3).

Figure 1. Typical barrio residential arrangement.

tical count. The relationship between adjacent families in the barrio as a whole is as frequently linked through females as through males. This judgment assumes that the criterion of interaction and adjacency is more important than sharing a single common patio area. If the more stringent criterion of sharing a common compound patio is invoked, then the ideally stated pattern of patrilocal residence has an edge of about two to one (i.e., about twice as many extended families are related only through males as there are extended families including both male and female adults).

A detailed examination of one or two residential arrangements will illustrate the organization of the extended family. Figures 1, 2, and 3 present a typical floor plan and the genealogies of some interrelated households.

An examination of Figure 1 illustrates several characteristic features of the compounds of the barrio as a whole. Note that there is no rigid pattern for the arrangement of the rooms and cook shacks within the compound area. This is true of the barrio as a whole, and an examination of the arrangement of all of the compounds in the barrio fails to reveal any two that are identical.

Despite the variety of arrangements, there are other characteristics that are true of almost all compound areas. There is always a common entrance from the street into the patio area. That is, members of the family can enter into the patio area, which is a common family

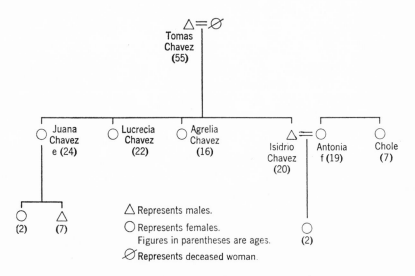

Figure 2. Genealogy of Chavez family.

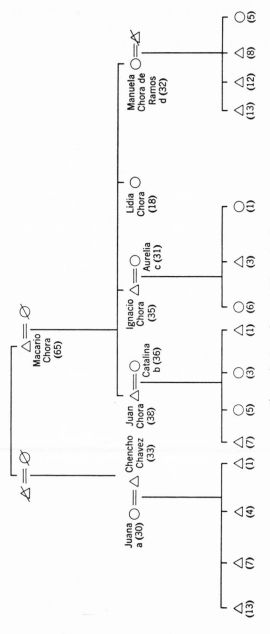

Figure 3. Genealogy of Chora family.

area, from the street without going through their individual rooms. In about 10% of the compounds in the barrio, there are additional private entrances. One private entrance illustrated in Figure 1 is the door from the street that goes directly into the living room of Juan Chora.

It is to be noted that each compound also contains cook shacks. The cook shacks in Figure 1 are all indicated as being round. This is generally the case, although some of them may be rectangular in shape. Also note that there is provision for a shed for animals in each of the compounds. In only one of the compounds illustrated in Figure 1 is there a well. In the barrio as a whole, approximately one out of ten compounds has a well.

The entrance from the patio area of Chencho Chavez into the room of Macario Chora and from there into the patio area of the main Chora compound indicates a rather close relationship between Chencho Chavez and the Chora family, and, in general, the compounds of closely related people may have common entry ways. This makes the problem of rigidly defining the boundary of a compound virtually impossible, and it illustrates the necessity for thinking of extended families in a flexible framework. As these families develop through time, it is possible for them to merge compounds or to partition a single compound into a series of smaller compounds. For example, on the large genealogy of the Chora family, it will be noted that Manuela Ramos is a sister of Juan and Ignacio Chora. As can be seen from the map, Manuela maintains a separate small patio area and cook shack. At one time Manuela's house was connected by an entry way to the common patio area of the Chora compound. Today we would have to consider her as occupying a distinct compound because there is no common entry way from her area into that occupied by her brothers. There is no set rule about when divisions of compounds might take place, and there are other compounds in the village in which married brothers and married sisters do live together in the same compound. Judged on the amount of interaction that takes place between Manuela's children and the children of Juan and Ignacio, Manuela's family could be considered part of the same extended family as her brothers.

The difficulty in distinguishing between closely related adjacent families is illustrated again in the position of Chencho Chavez, who is related to Juan and Ignacio as a cousin and who spends a good deal of time with his family in the compound area of Juan and Ignacio. (Chencho Chavez is more distantly related to Tomas Chavez and is living where he is because of his relationship to Macario Chora and not because of his relationship to the Chavez household.)

All adult women who have children who are not yet adults have cook shacks, as can be seen if we match up the genealogies to the cook shacks in the map. These are indicated in the figures with small letters. Elderly people—for example, Tomas and Macario—eat, in general, with the family of their eldest child if they live in the same compound. Thus Tomas Chavez eats with his daughter-in-law Antonia while Macario eats with the family of Juan Chora.

The ideal pattern of patrilocal residence probably influences the organization of the extended family in such cases as the families of Chencho and Manuela, both of whom are heads of households that are related through females, but neither of whom share the main Chora compound. However, there are several examples in the barrio of situations where an adult brother and sister do live in a common compound with their spouses and children. Thus the practice of separating the houses of brothers and sisters is not always carried out in the same way that it is in this particular family. Although much of the primary child care is allocated to a true sibling when one of an appropriate age and sex is available, one of the cousins frequently takes this responsibility when one is not available. Thus, for example, the children of the four families represented on the Chora genealogy in Figure 3 play together and have child caretaking responsibilities with very little differentiation between those who live in Manuela's family and those who live in the patio area of the main Chora family. This is not to say that there is no distinction, but only that the amount of interaction is very great and that the differences and distinctions made between the children who live within the compound and those who live in closely related compounds are very small from a child's point of view.

It is also important to remember that each of the individual nuclear families eats separately and that this is invariably the case throughout the barrio.

The internal organization of the extended family needs closer examination. We have seen that the extended family consists of a small number of nuclear families, together with various older people and a few other dependent relatives, as illustrated by the sister of Antonia in the Chavez family. Within the wider extended family, each nuclear family, consisting ideally of husband and wife and their children, occupies a distinct room and has use of a distinct cook shack. Thus, while there is a great deal of cooperation within the extended family, the individual nuclear families do maintain identity as separate and important social units. In the next chapter we will examine the functioning of these units as well as the complete family in its relations to the barrio as a whole. Let us return our attention now to further aspects of the internal organization of the families.

Economic arrangements within the family are best mirrored by the assignment of people to a particular cook shack. This defines the group that is economically responsible for food and its preparation. Though the children of a compound, or adjacent compounds, may play together in an undifferentiated way all day, and though the men may leave to go to the field, the nuclear family reassembles for major meals. In addition to the nuclear family, elderly people or younger dependent people will join a particular nuclear unit for purposes of eating. The food used by a particular woman in cooking is kept separate from that of all other women in the compound. For example, in the main Chora compound, Juan's wife is assigned one cook shack and Juan's father, Macario, eats with them, but their personal belongings and economic resources are kept separate from those of Juan's brother Ignacio. Lidia, an unmarried younger sister of Juan and Ignacio, eats with Ignacio. Thus we have a situation in which there are two adult couples who live in the same compound and share the use of the patio area and the shed for animals but who keep the produce of their fields separate from one another. In some compounds the woman who is economically responsible and occupies a cook shack may have no husband or male for support. An example of this situation is Juana Chavez in the Chavez household. Here, Juana is economically responsible for herself and her two younger sisters. They get some help from their brother Isidrio, but to a very great extent, they take care of themselves. In case of real economic need, families within the same extended household come to each other's aid, even though it is ideally stated that they are responsible for their own subsistence. The farmland belonging to an extended household is owned individually and not corporately. The houses within a compound are also individually owned. However, if a house is standing empty, its owner would certainly give permission for any close relative to occupy it and become a member of the extended family.

Thus, if an individual was in need, he would first turn to other members of his extended household for economic aid. If there were not enough resources within the extended family as a whole, he would appeal to close relatives in other extended households. There is a great deal of sharing of food and other resources within the extended family, but informal track is kept of the exchange of food and other items, and it is expected that the exchange will be reasonably equal.

One of the more important functions of the extended household is to increase the probability that an older child will be available for the caretaking of younger children. If we count all of the families in the barrio, we find that there are more cousins acting as caretakers of younger cousins than there are older siblings caring for younger siblings. Women with infants will also call on other women in the same extended household to care for their infants while they are away at market or otherwise occupied outside the compound area. So we find that the wife of Juan Chora will occasionally leave her youngest boy with the wife of Ignacio Chora. Sisters-in-law residing in a common household will even, on occasion, nurse each other's children or infants if necessary.

Older people within the extended family are respected but are not dictatorial heads of households. Thus, for example, Macario Chora and Tomas Chavez, in the households under discussion, are respected, but they do not give orders to their children and in many respects are dependent elderly males. They may not even be very active in work outside the household, but they would contribute the produce from any land they might have to the household in which they live and particularly to the group with which they eat.

There is no head, in any recognized or institutionalized sense, of the extended family as a whole. Rather, the adult men who are still in the prime of life all maintain more or less equal status, and each has complete freedom to carry on his affairs as he sees fit. The elder brother may have prerogatives in the community not yet obtained by the younger brother, but the elder brother does not have authority over the younger.

KINSHIP TERMINOLOGY

One of the indicators of family organization is the way in which people classify their relatives terminologically. The family organization in Santo Domingo is mirrored very nicely in the local kinship terminology. Figure 4 shows in diagrammatic form the way in which the barrio people classify their relatives. Each box in the diagram represents a category of relatives that are called by a single term. In each box we have included a crude English paraphrase for the kind of relative and have followed this with the Mixteco term in parentheses. The horizontal lines in the figure represent differences between generations, and the vertical lines represent distinctions made in terms of closeness of relationship. The closest relatives are direct relatives who stand in direct lines of ascent or descent or are full siblings. A second category is labeled collateral relatives, which includes the spouses

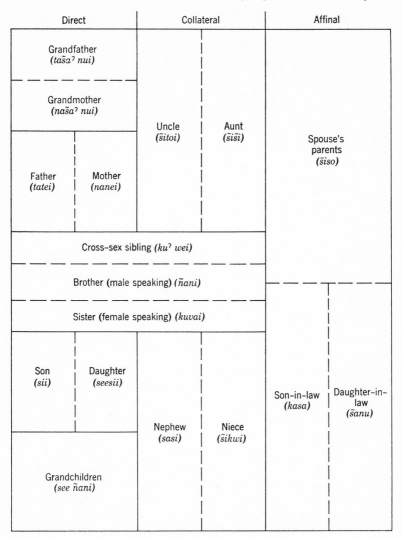

Figure 4. Kinship terminology of the barrio.

of collateral relatives and one's spouse's collateral relatives. The third major category includes one's wife's direct relatives and one's direct relative's spouses. Thus it can be seen that there is a single term for one's wife's mother and father and their parents, and, in turn, there are terms for one's children and their spouses. These last terms are further distinguished by sex.

A comparison of the Mixtec terminology to that in the United States reveals one major difference, together with a few minor differences. The major difference is that in the barrio siblings are not usually distinguished from cousins, while in the United States, we have separate terms for siblings and cousins. This reflects the emphasis given in the United States to the nuclear family. It is rare in our own society for one's cousins to be brought up in the same household, whereas in the barrio we have seen that a child almost always interacts frequently and closely with his cousins, generally in the same household. This terminological difference represents or symbolizes the fact that cousins are more like siblings in the barrio than in the United States, where a brother or sister is thought of as being very much closer than a cousin. Minor differences include the fact that in the barrio no distinction is made between the sex of grandchildren. Also, in the United States, we are more likely to distinguish great-aunt or great-uncle from aunt or uncle, and a grand-nephew or grand-niece from a nephew or niece. Another interesting difference is in the sibling and cousin terminology. Where English distinguishes only the absolute sex of the relative being referred to in the terms of brother and sister, the Mixtec system has three terms: one is used between relatives of opposite sex, that is, a male to his sister or female cousin and a female to her brother or male cousin, another is used between males, and still a third is used only between females.

One feature of the system is that although the term for cousin is the same as that for sibling, there is an optional addition of a modifier to distinguish them. In former times this option was never used and in everyday usage today it is still most common for this distinction to be ignored.

In terms of experience and contact with various relatives it is clear that, from a child's point of view, one plays in the compound with one's siblings and one's cousins and that little distinction in behavior is made between the two. This is reflected in the kinship terminology by the relatively minor and optional distinction between cousins and siblings. On the other hand, one looks to one's own parents for food and for the primary responsibility in caretaking and discipline. This is demonstrated in the eating patterns, in the sleeping patterns, and in the separate rooms for the nuclear families. Thus father and mother and son and daughter are closer than one's uncles and aunts and nephews and nieces. Since one's uncles and aunts from both sides of the family are likely to live close by with their spouses, one would not expect a distinction to be made between different kinds of aunts and uncles and whether they were related through blood or by marriage.

In this respect, the system is very similar to English. On the other hand, one's spouse's parents and one's children's spouses do not necessarily grow up in the same household; thus one assumes a new relationship with them upon their marriages, and they are clearly distinguished from other relatives.

There are no strongly patterned behaviorial preferences or customs among the barrio people. One is supposed to be helpful and responsible for one's relatives, but there are no taboos or strong patterns among relatives such as mother-in-law avoidance or joking relationship.

RITUAL KINSHIP AND FAMILY FIESTAS

As in many other parts of Mexico, ritual kinship is highly elaborated in the barrio. By far the most frequent term of address overheard on barrio streets is the term "compadre" or "comadre," indicating some kind of ritual kinship. There are nine occasions which result in ritual kinships. Ranked in order of most to least importance, they are as follows:

1. Baptism
2. First mass
3. First communion
4. Confirmation
5. Wedding
6. Raising of the cross after death
7. New house
8. Private saint
9. Animals (mainly for children)

Let us illustrate the concepts involved in this relationship by discussing baptism. When a child is born, the parents choose some couple they would like eventually to be the godparents of the new child. If the couple chosen agrees to the invitation, they become related by the term "padrinos." Padrinos are future godparents of the child and future compadres to the parents of the child. Unlike some systems in which the emphasis is placed on the godparent-godchild relationship, Santo Domingans put the emphasis on the compadre relationship, or the connection between the parents and godparents. The new padrinos then become responsible for certain duties such as arranging and paying for the baptism of their future godchild and providing a new set of clothes for the occasion. It is also their duty to supply a meal for the guests during the compadre ceremony.

Let us outline an actual example. One couple has an infant for whom it invites another couple to become godparents. The future godparents (padrinos) then arrange for the baptism. On the evening when the infant is to be baptized, there will be a procession to the church where the ceremony will take place. The padrinos go to the home of the parents, dress the infant in a new outfit, and carry the child to the church at the head of the procession. After the priest baptizes the child, the padrinos and guests return to the home of the parents of the infant, where food is served to everyone present, and then a ceremony is performed.

This ceremony consists of a series of speeches by a speaker representing the parents and another speaker for the padrinos in which the values of the ritual kinship tie are extolled. Ritual gifts are distributed between the two families. Afterward, the families and relatives of the parents line up opposite the families and relatives of the padrinos, and everyone in each line embraces everyone in the other line as they pass each other. It is on the occasion of the ceremonial embrace that the compadre relationship is solidified. After this ceremony, everyone who has taken part in the embraces calls each other "compadre." The padrinos have become compadres of the parents and godparents of the infant. The relationship between the infant and his godparents is permanent, and one is supposed to have respect for his godparents and be able to call on them in times of trouble, but the more significant relationship is the reciprocal one between compadres.

As can be seen, the proliferation of ritual kinship ties is very great in that the relatives of both parents and godparents also become ritually related.

There are regularities in the ceremonies in which ritual kinship ties are formed and in the duties performed by the actors in the ceremonies. Since all of these elements appear in the ceremonies connected with baptism, we may use it as an example in the following discussion. The ceremonial round that results in the formation of compadre relationships is always initiated by some person or persons in behalf of some occasion, object, or person(s). The initiating party is most frequently a married couple, in which case the initiative would be taken by the husband. Less frequently the initiative is taken by an individual.

The occasions that provide an appropriate setting for the initiating party to act are implied in the names of the kinds of compadre relationships listed previously. In the example of baptism, the parents of the new infant are the initiators in behalf of the infant. First mass, first communion, and confirmation are also appropriate occasions. In funeral ceremonies it is the cross which must be raised at the end of nine days that provides the appropriate object for the initiation of a compadre ceremony. The completion of a new house also sets the occasion for a couple to initiate a compadre ceremony.

Regardless of what sets the occasion for a compadre ceremony, the initiator's first action is to invite some person or persons to be padrinos of the object or event that sets the occasion for the ceremony. In the baptism ceremony they are said to be padrinos of the infant being baptized. In the case of a funeral they are padrinos of the cross. Similarly, there are padrinos of a new house and padrinos of private saints, and so forth. For baptism, first mass, first communion, and confirmation, a married couple is invariably chosen as padrinos. For a wedding two married couples are chosen, while for the funeral cross there are five, and for a new house, four. In the case of private saints and animals, only one couple is chosen.

For every ceremony the padrino has certain invariable responsibilities. For example, he always has the responsibility for "dressing" or caring for the object of which he is a padrino, for example, infant, cross, house, and so on. Thus, in the case of baptism, he supplies the clothes that the infant wears during the procession and baptism. For first mass or first communion or confirmation, the padrino would supply a new outfit of clothes. Similarly, for the wedding, the padrinos provide new clothes for the couple to be married. For the cross, house, saint, animals, and so on, the padrinos would be responsible for decorating or dressing the object.

A second invariable responsibility of the padrinos consists of arranging for a priest to bless the object or to carry out and consummate the ritual that constitutes the occasion for the ceremony. His services are needed on all the occasions and the padrinos arrange for his coming and pay for his services.

Another invariable aspect of the ceremony is that the padrinos and initiators of the ceremony must engage in the ritual meal. In almost all cases the meal follows the services of the priest. In a few cases where this is inconvenient or impossible, the meal may precede the services of the priest. In all cases in which the ritual meal follows the services, the ritual embrace takes place at that time. Otherwise it will take place after the services.

All of the above features are invariable, even though they may occur in rather attenuated form. For example, the ritual meal may not consist of anything more than hot chocolate and sweet bread. Features in the ceremony that are subject to variation include the size and elaborateness of the ceremony, whether or not speakers for the two sides are formally chosen and participate in the ceremony, as well as the number of padrinos involved in the ceremony. Two examples in addition to the one given on baptism may aid in giving an idea of the amount of variation and importance invested in the *compadre* relationship. We will discuss those connected with animals and with the completion of a new house.

During February of each year a special day is set aside for the blessing of animals by the local priest. On these occasions, if a youth or older child desires to form a compadre relationship with a friend, he may do so by inviting the friend to be a padrino of an animal. If the friend accepts, it becomes his responsibility as padrino of the animal to dress and decorate the animal with crepe paper and ribbons and to carry it down to the central part of town where it is blessed by the priest. Then the padrino of the animal returns the animal to the house of its owner, and the children or youths have a meal together and go through the ritual embrace and become compadres. The resulting relationship is not necessarily permanent and tends to be recognized only so long as the participants find it convenient. It is discussed here to illustrate the total range of compadre relationships that is possible. The animal involved may be a pet or farm animal; it does not matter. The mood surrounding this little ritual is as playful as it is serious. It is taken very lightly by adults. However, it is exceedingly popular, and the central church courtyard is always full of a weird collection of animals, ranging from birds to bulls, on the day designated for the blessing of the animals by the local priest.

The compadre relationship is also formed when a new house is completed. In this situation the owner of the house invites four people to be padrinos of the house, that is, future compadres. These padrinos decorate (dress) the house and arrange for the priest to come and bless it, following which there are a ritual meal and the ceremony involving the ritual embrace between the family who owns the house and the families of the padrinos. All who embrace thereby become compadres.

Some general remarks on ritual kinship may be useful. It is significant to note that it is the collateral tie between compadres that is stressed and not the lineal tie between godparents and godchild. This is a very dominant theme in the barrio and is consistent with the annual circulation of membership in the cofradias. The custom of having someone speak for the principals during the ritual corresponds to the practice in the cofradias of a speaker for the mayordomo. The term padrino is also used reciprocally between future compadres.

It should be pointed out that the importance placed on a compadre relationship varies with the importance of the original occasion which gave rise to the association, baptism being the most important and the blessing of animals, the least important. For the more important type of compadre relationships, the children of compadres would extend terms for brothers and sisters to each other. Consequently, if you heard two men call each other brother, it may mean that their parents are close compadres or it may mean that they are in fact brothers or cousins. The compadre relationship is the one that is frequently called on when one needs more labor than can be supplied by one's true relatives. If a man needs help in putting up a house, he may call on his compadres to help him; or if a man needs many helpers during harvest, he will call on his compadres. In these situations he will pay for food and refreshment after the task is done. There is no exchange of money for these kinds of services.

In addition to the fiestas involving compadre relationships, there are a small number of occasions for which it is appropriate to give private fiestas. The main kinds of private fiestas are those for harvesting a field, for celebrating one's birthday, and for celebrating the anniversary of the death of an important relative. On any of these occasions it is appropriate to give a large meal for everyone involved and to serve aguardiente. The harvesting of fields is almost invariably accompanied by a private fiesta at the end of the day's work. Birthdays are frequently celebrated in a similar way, as is the anniversary of the death of a parent or, more rarely, of a spouse.

✢
✢
✢

Chapter 5

Barrio Social Organization

The most important set of customs relating to social organization in the barrio is the "cofradia" organization. A cofradia is a society organized for the purpose of sponsoring celebrations in honor of various saints. In Santo Domingo a cofradia refers to a group of people who are organized into a society whose function it is to honor a particular saint. Most of the cofradias hold a celebration on that saint's day; in addition, they hold a midyear celebration. Other cofradias may honor the saint for a whole month.

An example of the first type of cofradia is that organized to honor Santiago, the patron saint of Juxtlahuaca. The largest ceremony of the year is held during the days preceding and following July 25th, the day of Santiago. The midyear celebration on January 25th is a smaller ceremony, also sponsored by the cofradia, to honor Santiago. An example of a cofradia that involves no large celebration but honors a particular saint for a longer period of time is one called Heart of Jesus. This is celebrated during the whole month of June, with a special mass on June 29th.

The cofradias are composed of groups of varying numbers of people, from as few as 3 or 4 to as many as 40 or 50. Each cofradia has a leader or mayordomo. The mayordomo, as well as the rest of the members, or diputados, of the cofradia, serves for a period of one year. It is the duty of the mayordomo and his helpers to sponsor a celebration to honor the saint for whom that cofradia has responsibility. The celebrations may vary from year to year, depending on how much economic surplus the community may have. In years of drought the celebration in honor of the patron saint Santiago may be fairly small, while in good years the celebration would be very large.

There is a total of nine cofradias in the barrio; thus, including midyear celebrations, there would be approximately 18 fiestas in honor of saints during the year. Not all of these celebrations would be participated in by all the members of the barrio, but approximately five or six during the year are important enough to involve everyone, and some would include invited guests from several of the surrounding Mixtec villages. The nine cofradias in the barrio are listed below in approximate order of importance.

1. Santiago
2. Santo Domingo
3. San Sebastian
4. San Marcos
5. Padre Jesus
6. Santa Cruz
7. Virgin of the Rosario
8. Heart of Jesus
9. Heart of Mary

The first six mentioned above are all composed of men, while the last three are made up entirely of women. The activties of the women's groups differ slightly from those of the men's groups. For example, the duties of the female cofradias extend through a whole month, during which time the women place flowers in the church daily and arrange for special masses. Those cofradias composed of men give celebrations centering on a particular saint's day, as well as the mid-year celebrations.

The functioning of the major cofradias can best be understood by referring to a specific example. We will describe the celebration sponsored by the cofradia responsible for honoring the day of the patron saint of Juxtlahuaca, Santiago. The fiesta we observed had been preceded by a year of good crops and was considered a relatively large one. The mayordomo was assisted by 45 helpers. While the main day of the celebration was July 25th, the program participated in by all barrio members and people from several other towns included the five days from July 24th to July 28th. Some weeks before the main festivities began, the cofradia sent out invitations to surrounding villages to invite their musical and dancing groups to participate in the celebration. In addition, they invited the members of 12 of the surrounding Mixtec villages to come as guests.

The celebration is always financed by contributions, in decreasing amounts, from the mayordomo, his helpers, and guests. For this one, the mayordomo contributed 1500 pesos, each of his helpers contributed the equivalent of 250 pesos, either in the form of money or goods, while guests contributed 3 pesos. All of these contributions are classed as voluntary donations. It may be noted parenthetically that any time an individual in the barrio accumulates any money, great pressures are put on him to participate in an important cofradia either as a helper or as a mayordomo. When one considers that the average income of a barrio male is about 3 pesos a day, one can understand the extent of the economic sacrifice made by a mayordomo and his diputados.

When a mayordomo or helper is chosen to serve in a cofradia, his participation is considered voluntary and includes not only the services and contributions of the male but also the contributions of his family. Each member of the cofradia is responsible for furnishing several days' work on the part of his wife. In the vast majority of cases, it is only married men who participate as helpers or mayordomo in the cofradia. If a man does not have a wife, one of his relatives will serve in place of the wife.

This fiesta in celebration of Santiago is considered an Indian celebration, and the townspeople do not attend except for a token appearance at the dances and music during the major days. Beginning on the 17th of July and continuing to the 25th, special masses are given in the church each day. Each of these masses is arranged, sponsored, and paid for by a particular member of the barrio as a contribution to the over-all celebration in honor of the patron saint.

As we observed on July 24th, the musical groups and guests began to arrive and to congregate at the community house of the barrio. A musical group or band consisting of several wind instruments, together with a drum and fife and violin, came from each of four villages. Thus, by 10 o'clock in the morning there were five musical groups playing music in the community center. The music continued for five days with no time out during the evening. The groups took turns, but one or another played day and night for the five days. In addition, four dancing groups—Chareos, Chilolos, Rubios, and Moros—assembled and provided entertainment for the guests during most of the daylight hours. These groups consist of from 5 to 30 members, all in costume, and each group performs a kind of dramatic story. The dance of the Moros, for example, consists of two lines of dancers facing each other, dancing forward and back, swinging their machetes as swords, re-enacting the fight between the Christians and the Moros. All of these dances date from the colonial period in Mexico, when they were introduced by the Spaniards, and have since evolved from these early dramatic dance forms.

The middle of the day of the 24th, the music had begun playing and the dancers had each given a performance. Then a procession was organized with the mayordomo and his helpers at the head, followed by the band and dance groups, with the guests bringing up the rear. This procession, preceded by fireworks and other festive activities, went to the barrio church. At the church the image of the patron saint, which is a figure approximately 5 feet high of Santiago seated on a horse, was removed from the church, and a benediction in his honor was delivered by the priest in the churchyard. A smaller image, approximately 2 inches high and made of silver, was also blessed. Then the larger image was returned to its position in the church while the smaller image was carried by the procession to the courtyard and house of the mayordomo, where it would stay for the remainder of the celebration. In the courtyard of the mayordomo, the musicians continued to play and the dance groups to perform while the helpers went to their respective homes to gather together their contributions for the festivities. During the course of the afternoon, turkeys, chickens, and cattle to be used for food later in the ceremony were gathered together in the mayordomo's courtyard. Around 4 o'clock in the afternoon, these animals and other foods had been assembled and decorated.

The mayordomo, his family, and friends carrying his contributions, followed by the helpers with their families and contributions, made up another procession, which returned to the community center. The year that we observed this procession there were 3 beef cattle, 80 turkeys, and 50 chickens, together with numerous gallons of aguardiente and many bags of cocoa beans and other foodstuffs.

On returning to the community center, the men of the cofradia, together with their wives, immediately began the slaughter of all of the animals and the preparation of the food. In the evening at the community center a meal was served to all the assembled people, and the dances and fireworks and music continued on into the evening.

During all the time the celebration was going on at the community center, the males composing the cofradia sat inside the large community room around a single, very long table. It is their duty to sit there, to make speeches, and to eat and drink during all five days of the ceremony. They leave the room only to participate in the processions and the masses, and they catch what sleep they can while sitting at the table.

The second day, July 25th, which is the major day, is primarily focused around a religious procession in which the large image of Santiago is paraded completely around the village of Juxtlahuaca. Stops are made at each of the four corners of the village, and the saint is placed inside a previously prepared temporary shelter in which an altar has been arranged. The priest blesses the saint at each of these stops. This is one of the processions in which townspeople participate to a much greater extent than they do in the others. In the early afternoon after this religious procession, the main banquet takes place. The beef slaughtered the night before is served with mole and specially baked bread and other festive foods. The evening is devoted to a special church service, after which the major fireworks and dancing resume in the community center.

The third day of the fiesta continues the dancing and music and eating of the preceding days, with one additional special event. This event is a ritual meeting between the officials of the Spanish-speaking part of town and the barrio officials. During this special ceremony the presidente or mayor of the town, together with other town officials, meets with the Indian officials of the barrio and the cofradia inside the community house. Official greetings are brought by the mayor and his group to the barrio officials. An exchange of gifts is made between the two groups, and several speeches are made in which the recurring theme is the maintenance of good relations between the two parts of the community. The cofradia is represented by a specially designated speaker, not by the mayordromo himself. The mayor of the town reaffirms his delegation of certain authority and independence to the barrio officials. In turn, the barrio officials reaffirm their willingness to obey the laws and customs of the town. Town and barrio groups of men are then served a special meal by the wives of the helpers, after which the town officials depart and the general festivities continue.

The following two days of the fiesta continue with music and dancing during the day and some fireworks at night. Inside the community house, the men devote themselves to the business of choosing a new set of helpers for the cofradia for the following year. They also have to make an accounting of the finances and belongings of the cofradia, and they go through a ceremony to transfer these belongings and responsibilities to the new mayordomo and his helpers. On the last day there is a procession from the home of the old mayordomo to the home of the new, and the new mayordomo and his helpers then officially take over the duties for honoring the saint for the coming year.

The preceding description of a ceremony given by a cofradia should give the reader some idea of the nature of the ceremony. Let us call attention to a few of the more salient and general features of the ceremony as a whole. That it is a ceremony in which the Indian barrio takes great pride is apparent. That the barrio holds these kinds of ceremonies while the townspeople do not sets it off as distinctively Indian. That a ceremony as large as this one is a significant economic drain on the part of the community that can least afford it is also noteworthy. Clearly, such a fiesta pattern makes it impossible for the Indians to accumulate any amount of capital. The men in the barrio view membership in a cofradia as both a duty and an honor. However, the way in which the men cooperate to produce such a celebration makes it impossible, also, for any single person to maintain any special prestige or privileges. The fact that a new group of men takes over each year means that each adult male in the barrio will have served in several cofradias during the course of his life. If a cofradia gives a particularly successful celebration, people will talk about it for a few years, but no other rewards are entailed.

Thus the honoring of a patron saint is seen as reflecting on the barrio as a whole and not as raising any individual above any others. The behavior of the cofradia meetings is democratic and equalitarian. The same thing is true of the women's behavior in the preparation of food in that no one woman directs the activities of the others; instead, they all do their part without prompting or direction.

Many of the ceremonies are rather small and may include only

200 or 300 people in the barrio; but a general feature of all cofradia ceremonies is the inclusion of music, dancing, drinking, and serving of a meal. These items are a minimum requirement in the celebration of any saint's day by a cofradia.

☘

☘

☘

Chapter 6

Social Control

Social control mechanisms may be defined as the various devices used by a society to ensure conformity to the rules of the society and to control the aggressive impulses of its members. Uncontrolled aggression would pose a serious threat to the social organization of the barrio. The discussion of social control will emphasize the control of aggression among adults.

Before describing reaction to physical aggression and occasions that may lead to aggression, it is important to point out that the more serious crimes, such as homicide, would be handled within the framework of the regular court systems in Mexico. The following discussion focuses on the mechanisms used within the barrio to minimize aggressive outbursts. No attempt will be made to describe the wider court system of Mexico as it is practiced in the central part of town.

It is rare for a conflict between members of the barrio to reach the Mexican court system. Conflicts do arise between members of the barrio and townspeople, and these frequently reach the formal court system. This is partly because the townspeople are not under the influence of the factors operating within the barrio to reduce aggression and conflict.

No barrio member was involved in a court case during our year's residence in the field. No cases of theft nor accusations of theft came to our attention, and despite the fact of numerous opportunities, the investigators never lost any material goods during the year. Adultery between members of the barrio does not reach the formal court system but is handled within the barrio, as will be reported below. On the other hand, if a person from the center of town were to attack a barrio girl, it is reported that her family may well take the case to court; otherwise there would be no possible way of punishing the offender or receiving justice.

During a year's study in Juxtlahuaca, we observed only one case of overt physical aggression among members of the barrio. This particular episode will be described in some detail, for it illustrates many salient points. It took place during a group house-building fiesta in which the roof of a house was being completed by a group of approximately 20 men, while the women were gathered around the cook shack preparing food to be served when the task was completed. Several men were on the roof of the house passing up tiles; several others were on the ground carrying materials and handing them up to those on the roof.

The task was just about completed, and the men had begun to drink; the bottle of aguardiente was being passed with some frequency. A young man named Pedro was drinking somewhat more heavily than the others while engaged in placing tiles at the very edge of the roof. A certain amount of by-play in the form of verbal joking was going on in a good-natured way with Pedro as a particularly prominent participant. As the drinking and bantering gained in momentum and the task neared completion, two or three men began pointing out to Pedro that his work was getting a little sloppy. They invited him to get off the roof and stop working and indicated that they would join him presently.

At one point a couple of men corrected Pedro's work by replacing some tiles. Pedro objected to this and said that he was perfectly capable of placing the tiles. While the men tried to humor him, he slipped and fell from the roof. His falling from the roof was not caused by any kind of physical scuffling; it was an accident caused by Pedro's partial drunkenness and by his tripping. When he fell to the ground, a fall of about 10 feet, people first looked to see whether or not he was hurt, and then everyone laughed uproariously. Nothing was hurt but Pedro's pride, and he wanted to climb back up on the roof and work.

At this point two or three men attempted physically to stop him and to humor him into staying on the ground. Pedro struck out at the men who were trying to prevent him from going back on the roof. The response of the men whom he struck was to move back and to try to cajole him into complying with their wishes. It was also clear that there was consensus among the men that Pedro had had enough to drink, that his effectiveness as a workman was impaired, and that it would be better if he sat quietly for a period of time. The men backed away to the street adjacent to where they were working; Pedro followed them and tried to pick a fight by hitting one or two of the men with his fists. None of the other men returned the blows, and several of them, including his closest friends, crowded around and put their hands on Pedro's shoulders, attempting to calm him down. He continued in his aggressive manner for three or four minutes, and all of the men became very anxious to quiet him. Finally, two of his friends persuaded him to sit down and take it easy and to forget further work.

There are several things to note in the above episode. One is the typical pattern of beginning to drink just before a task is finished, in anticipation of the food and drink which invariably follow work groups of this sort. The second thing is that none of the men returned Pedro's blows. Yet another point to notice is the fact that the men saw humor in the clumsiness of Pedro's falling from the roof. This is a very typical reaction on the part of male adults in particular and, to a lesser extent, of female adults in the barrio. We will note in the discussion of socialization that the reaction of an adult to a child's falling or accidentally hurting himself changes from nurturance to ridicule at the particular stage that marks the boundary between early childhood and late childhood. Another thing to stress is the amount of concern shown by all of the men for Pedro's aggression. They were clearly disturbed and wanted to do everything possible to calm him down and to avoid any aggressive behavior.

When interviewed afterward about the cause of Pedro's aggression, the men reported that this was extremely unusual behavior. They remarked that Pedro had gone to the city to work in the past and there had picked up the habit of smoking marijuana. During the morning of this occasion, he had been smoking marijuana; and, in their opinion, it was only a combination of the marijuana and drinking that could give rise to and account for such aggressive behavior. They reported that there were two other individuals in the barrio who had picked up the habit of smoking marijuana and that this was a particularly bad habit. Although they seemed to feel that it was a person's own business, they did consider that it was sad and unfortunate when such a thing happened.

When informants were asked about other causes of aggression, they reported that in the past, women, political factions, and land disputes were the most usual causes of aggression.

They reported that men sometimes fought over women but that this was very rare. There were no cases of men resorting to physical aggression over women during the year that we were there, and most reported episodes had taken place at some time in the past. If a man discovers that his wife has been sleeping or flirting with another man, his aggression may be taken out, according to informants, on either the other man or the wife. Although they did not remember any recent examples, they reported occasions when men beat their wives for sleeping with other men. They also reported episodes, again none recent, of men fighting over women. There was one case that was remembered from an earlier generation of a man being killed in a fight over women. During the field period we had occasion to learn of cases in which a barrio wife was known to be sleeping with another man, but there was no physical aggression as a result. On one occasion we actually observed an informant discover another man in bed with his wife, and his response was to shrug his shoulders and to walk around the block. We do not know what happened subsequently, although we never observed or heard of any repercussions. On another occasion we observed an episode involving a married man and an unmarried woman who were discovered in bed together. This fact became common knowledge in the barrio, and the result was a good deal of gossip directed toward both the man and the woman. Two days later, the woman went to stay with some relatives in Mexico City for a period of a month until the gossip had died down. The man remained in the barrio, and, other than gossip, there were no observable repercussions in his relation to his wife and family and to the other members of the barrio.

During election years the people in the center of town are extremely active and acrimonious in the political campaigns. Although the Indians in the barrio have relatively little political power, several of the men are able to exert their right to vote. During this time emotions ride high and are fanned by the more aggressive people of the town, where physical aggression in the form of fights between men is not unusual. Any and all means of political persuasion are used during campaigns, including economic pressure and threats in the form of ambush and shooting by the townspeople. The political leaders in town attempt to attract the more progressive male adults from the barrio to their side and urge them to proselyte in their behalf. On these occasions it is reported that barrio men will sometimes find themselves in opposite factions and that, in the past, this has led to fighting among barrio members. Our field session took place during an election year, and it was apparently a quiet one, for there was no physical aggression in the form of fights generated in either the barrio or the town, but the informants reported that it is more normal for the townspeople to get into fights than not. The general attitude among the more level-headed elders in the barrio is to advocate noninvolvement in the political affairs of the main part of town, and there is a great deal of gossip to the effect that it is bad to get overinvolved in politics.

The problem of land disputes is a recurring one and most frequently pits the barrio men against the townspeople, although on occasion there can be disputes between members of the barrio concerning privately owned irrigated land in the valley.

One of the possible causes of aggression, which was specifically denied by informants on direct questioning, is drinking. This corresponds to our observations at the fiesta, where the men generally drank a great deal during the ceremonies but were never observed to become loud or aggressive.

We observed that the barrio people conform rather closely to their customs and are relatively free of aggressive outbursts and serious crimes. Two interrelated questions arise from such observations. First, how is such conformity to the group's standards maintained, and, second, how are the aggressive impulses so effectively controlled? Several very powerful social control mechanisms are at work in the barrio. The remainder of this chapter will be devoted to describing these mechanisms and attempting to interpret their success.

One approach to an understanding of why barrio members are so conforming and nonaggressive is to analyze the various types of possible punishments or threats of punishments for nonconformity, including aggressive outbursts. Many societies have a mechanism for imposing fines, jail sentences, or physical punishment for crimes against the society or its members. There are no such mechanisms within the barrio, and the barrio members seldom resort to the formal courts which do use such punishments. Thus the threat of such things as fines or jail sentences is not a primary mechanism of social control within the barrio. Still other societies use mechanisms such as gossip, backbiting, or threats of sorcery as mechanisms for social control. It is true that there is a certain amount of gossip within the barrio, and beliefs about sorcery do exist. However, the gossip is not of a very malicious nature, nor it is a preoccupation among the people. Similarly, almost no people in the barrio believe that they have been victims of sorcery. No one in the barrio is thought to be a sorcerer. Even though most of them believe that sorcerers exist in other villages, they are not preoccupied with the menace of sorcery. Thus such mechanisms as fear of sorcery, fear of malicious gossip or backbiting, or fear of physical punishment will not account for the degree of conformity observed in the barrio. We must look for other mechanisms of social control.

We believe that ostracism from the social life of the barrio is one of the realistic threats for compelling conformity and one of the important mechanisms of social control. Participation in the social life of the barrio and social acceptance are particularly important to the barrio individual. Emphasis on collateral ties is greatly elaborated in the family and social organization of the barrio, and the threat of ostracism would constitute an important deterrent on an individual's behavior.

One of the values in barrio social life is participation in the fiestas sponsored by the cofradias. During these fiestas the men sit in the main room of the community house and engage in social drinking. The drinking patterns during this time (and some observed deviations) provide insight into the importance of ostracism as a mechanism of social control. The pattern of drinking is highly stylized and has high symbolic meaning to the people of the barrio. We will describe it in some detail because of its importance in its contribution to understanding the role of ostracism.

As soon as the men congregate in the community room on any official confradia fiesta, a speaker for the mayordomo will stand and make a welcoming speech. The speech always contains references to the cohesiveness of the barrio group and to the necessity for maintaining ritual and ceremonial continuity with the past. At the end of his speech he invites the mayordomo to drink with him. A tray with two shot glasses on it is handed to the speaker, and he fills both of them with aguardiente. The speaker and mayordomo then salute each other and down the drinks in one gulp. It is obligatory for them to finish the entire shot. The tray is then passed on to the next individual at the table, and he salutes his neighbor at the table in the same way. The tray with the glasses and the bottle is passed around the entire table in this manner. There is a large bottle containing several gallons of aguardiente in the corner of the room, and each time the small bottle is emptied, it is replenished. It is obligatory for each man to drink with his neighbor at the table. In case one does not finish the entire amount of aguardiente, his penalty is that the glass must be refilled and he must drink again. There are no customs that allow an individual under these circumstances to refuse a drink. This differs from customs in other parts of Mexico where one may take the drink and pour it into his own bottle to save it until later or take only a sip, symbolizing his acceptance of the drink. By the time the tray reaches the head of the table and everyone has had one drink, another speech will have been made, and the tray will then make another round. This continues all during the time of the fiesta, which means that, for a small cofradia celebration, it will continue for a period of 12 hours or so; but, for a large fiesta, the men may be drinking, practically day and night, for a period of three days or longer. The result is that every man drinks either very close to his capacity or, more commonly, beyond it. It is perfectly acceptable for an individual to pass out at the table, and it is rather common during the longer fiestas. During the time that a man is unconscious, he is passed in the round of drinking; however, when he comes to and sits back up to the table, he is obligated to take his turn when the bottle is passed around.

The manifest function of this drinking pattern as stated by the men is that it represents solidarity and acceptance within the group. They recognize that the pattern is very different from that in the central part of town and say that it sets the Indian off from the Mexican. They also say that it symbolizes acceptance of the Indians and of the whole cofradia organization and the round of fiestas that it entails.

As an outsider we might interpret this pattern as having an aggressive as well as a sociable function. If we ask the question as to who is being aggressive to whom, the only answer is that a group of peers are being mutually aggressive among themselves. In this sense it is a high price to pay in order to stay in the round of ceremonies at the bario-wide level represented by the cofradias. To the extent that it does function as a mechanism for peers to dominate peers in a self-reciprocal type of way, it is a covert and unrecognized mechanism. The men would certainly deny that it had any aggressive or mutually dominating function.

Two other aspects warrant examination. One of these is the function of drink in other contexts and the second, more important, is the question as to what happens if a person is unwilling or unable to participate in such a round of drinking. The question concerning the use of alcohol in other contexts will be answered first. In other ceremonial contexts, for example, compadre ceremonies or private parties such as birthdays or harvest parties, alcohol is used in much the same way it is in the cofradia ceremonies. There is less drinking, with a few exceptions which would include weddings, where a great deal of alcohol is consumed. However, the patterns of reciprocal drinking are pretty much the same in other fiesta contexts, although not quite so formalized; the bottle is not passed around in a definite order, but most individuals drink about the same amount, and if invited to drink on these occasions, they must accept.

Outside of the fiesta context, the barrio men almost never drink aguardiente or other alcoholic beverages. There is one marginal person in the barrio who does drink in nonfiesta contexts, but he is not a full member of the barrio. He is the one individual who is not engaged in farming as a primary occupation and who is a marginal person in many other respects. Aside from this man, only a few of the younger barrio men drink in nonfiesta contexts and then only rarely. Thus the prevailing pattern for the consumption of alcohol is to drink very heavily in the fiesta context and not at all between times. Questioned about whether or not they desired alcohol between fiestas, the men in the barrio always responded as though this were a peculiar question because obviously one drank only during fiesta occasions. Most of the men accepted this drinking pattern as the only natural and imaginable one possible. A few of the very elderly men reported that they thought there was too much drinking at the fiestas.

Alcohol, or aguardiente, is used in one or two ritual contexts. For example, before a field is planted it is used to feed the earth god and is poured in each corner of the field. In summary, aguardiente is used almost exclusively in a social context, either between men or between man and spirit. It thus has acquired a high social, symbolic value and represents social solidarity at the conscious level for barrio people.

The second question concerns what happens when an individual is unwilling or unable to drink during the ceremonies. There are three or four men in the barrio who claim, for physiological reasons, that they are unable to drink aguardiente. These men are all excluded from attending any cofradia function. Two of them had been highly respected men with important roles in cofradia organization in the past. They were now ostracized from such participation. None of these men had the full respect of other barrio members, nor were they considered to be full-fledged members of the barrio. When referred to by other barrio people, they were frequently classed as being closer to the townspeople. In addition, they clearly paid a price in terms of being deprived of the emotional and economic security afforded by barrio members. It will be remembered that the cofradia fiestas are the major occasions on which every member of the barrio eats meat and other special fiesta foods, so that the economic function of food distribution is withheld from the families of the men who do not drink.

The threat of ostracism is one important way of ensuring participation in the barrio-wide cofradia organizations. It would be invoked primarily as a punishment for not conforming to the ritual aspects of the cofradia ceremonies, particularly participation in the ceremonial drinking pattern. The threat of ostracism does not seem adequate, however, to account for the degree of control of overt aggression observed within the barrio. It does not account, for example, for the lack of any great aggressiveness in the ceremonies themselves. Another mechanism relating to aggression remains to be discussed.

The low level of overt aggression observed among the barrio members may be accounted for, at least in part, by two factors. The first factor consists of the training in the control of aggression during childhood. This will be discussed at length in Part II. The second factor has to do with a set of beliefs concerning aggression. These beliefs will be the concern of the remainder of the chapter.

Members of the barrio share an elaborated set of beliefs concerning the relationship between aggression and illness. Anger, aggression, jeolousy, and related kinds of emotions are believed capable of causing illness which may result ultimately in death. These beliefs are very strongly held and are related to the stress on self-control of aggressive impulses.

The way in which these beliefs account for various kinds of phenomena may be best illustrated by the examination of a case history from field notes. It concerned a woman, whom we shall call Catalina, who supplemented her income by selling tortillas in the market place. All people who occupy any space in the market are expected to pay a very small tax for the space they occupy there. One market day when Catalina was selling her tortillas, the tax collector came around to her place in the market to collect the tax. By mistake, he attempted to collect the tax a second time from her. She tried to explain that she had already paid her tax, and an argument of a very mild nature ensued. Shortly afterward, she confided to her friends in the market that she had felt very angry about this double imposition and that she did not feel well and was worried about having become so angry. She thereupon left the market in the afternoon and went home. She became increasingly ill during the evening and died about midnight. The cause of her death was attributed to the illness that was caused by her aggressive feelings. All of the people in the barrio accepted this as the explanation. The event was reported to the children and talked about in front of them and used as an object lesson for the importance of controlling one's feelings.

The well-internalized belief that anger or aggression can lead to illness and possibly death is a strong deterrent to placing oneself in a situation that may lead to anger or aggression. When the validity of such a belief is reinforced or demonstrated by actual deaths, as in the case of Catalina, it becomes a very potent deterrent to aggressive behavior and thoughts.

＊
＊
＊

Chapter 7

Disease and Curing

Illness is common in the barrio. Although some of it is chronic (for example, rheumatism, certain types of dysentery, and malaria among those men who have worked in hot country), much illness is seasonal. The winter months bring colds and flu with their complications (earache, eye inflammation), especially among children. Measles strike yearly in the heat of the spring before the rains begin, and here again children are the principal victims. In the rainy summer months intestinal diseases are common. Barrio people recognize the seasonal distribution of kinds of illness to some extent by their tendency to lay the blame for an epidemic on the weather. For example, one woman explained the occurrence of much illness one summer by saying that in the previous year the rains had come earlier, and so by June the water was no longer muddy and there was little sickness. The association of muddy water and sickness in her thinking seems likely. April and May are said to be good months for taking a purgative, perhaps to prepare for the dangers of summer. Again, measles is said to occur at about the same time each year, when the sun is so hot that it heats the blood and produces a rash as the heat seeks a way out of the body.

Although the weather helps to explain the widespread occurrence of illness in the barrio, the illness of an individual is usually thought to have much more specific causes. Some few conditions—for example, wounds, burns, poison ivy, and malaria—are believed to be caused by the physical agents with which they are associated in Western medicine. Poison ivy is contracted by touching or being near the plant, and malaria comes from the bite of a mosquito in hot country. Most diseases, however, are assigned causes of other kinds. In order of importance, these include: (1) disturbed emotional states such as fear and anger, (2) ritual contamination, (3) magical seizure by sorcery, and (4) improper diet or regimen. Supplementing these categories in the ex-

planation of individual illness is the belief in differential susceptibility to illness. Susceptibility is increased by abnormal bodily conditions brought about by exertion, excessive sweating, body exposure,
wounds or blows, as well as by the conditions of pregnancy, parturition,
menstruation, and menopause. Weakness may also be due to extreme
youth or to old age. The illness of a particular individual is interpreted in the light of his condition (weakness or strength) and his
recent experience, as well as his symptoms.

Fright is "like a heat in the stomach," taking away the appetite and
producing fever, sleeplessness, and general apathy. It may follow a fall,
especially a fall into water, or the unexpected sight of a snake, or any
other event which produces fear or shock. (Among these other events
is the sight of aggression, "seeing some person kill another person,
or seeing someone else pushing somebody from behind into the water.")
Anger as well as sometimes causing illness and sometimes death is also
believed to cause pain in childbirth and miscarriage in those who
are weak for one reason or another. One type of weakness which is
relevant here is an overabundance of bile or, rather, a tendency for the
bile to be discharged readily into the stomach or the liver. The danger
of illness following anger is greatest before breakfast because the bile
sack is fullest then. It is considerably less after eating, for then food
supports the sack, and the bile is less likely to be released. Another
type of weakness is due to pregnancy, which entails the danger of pain
or miscarriage. Still another is due to menstruation, which makes the
pores hollow due to loss of blood.

Ritual contamination may cause excessive crying in an infant, illness (fever and vomiting), or bodily deformity. It comes from a number of sources. One of the most common is the evil eye. People who
have unusually bright, staring, or hypnotic eyes are thought to cause
illness or harm merely by looking at another person. It is possible for
this person to contaminate the individual unconsciously as he (or, more
frequently, she) admires him, but some cases of evil eye are said to
have been deliberately caused by a witch. Infants are particularly
vulnerable to the evil eye, especially when they are sleeping and hence
defenseless. Another kind of contamination is *mal aire,* a term which
includes two rather different concepts. One is simply evil air, which
may enter the body and cause illness. Gas in the intestines is interpreted as "air inside" and is a cause of worry and loss of appetite in
many barrio people. Night air is evil, and people go outdoors at night
rarely and then with nose and mouth covered by the rebozo or serape.

The second concept translated as *mal aire* is a dark shape which
may be encountered at night. This shape frightens the victim, and

fright is formally the cause of the resulting symptoms. However, the symptoms—fainting, dizziness, "absence of breathing," half-consciousness—are quite different from the usual result of fright. The same symptoms are reported for the result of an encounter with the *tabayuku*, or owner of the earth. The *tabayuku* appears only to men, and always in the shape of a woman—the particular woman whom the man is thinking about at the moment, whether wife or lover or someone else. The *tabayuku* takes the victim to her cave and kisses him. She offers the victim many wonderful things—all the things he has wanted—and asks that the victim pay her for them with a kiss. Afterward the victim returns home half-crazed, and unless he is cured, he may die.

Evil air also emanates from the body of a dead person. It can cause a swelling on the back of the head of a newborn infant if either he or his mother is exposed to it.

Sorcery can cause insanity as well as other forms of illness. It is sometimes used by one person who is angry with another. The person who bears the grudge does not do the witchcraft himself. Instead, he hires a witch in el Centro or, more often, in one of the neighboring towns. (There are said to be no witches in the barrio.) The witch may steal the soul of the victim by sending out his *nagual*, or animal counterpart, and illness results. Alternatively, the witch may make a small figure of wax or clay in the shape of the victim and stick cactus spines into it. The figure may have an opening where the stomach would be, into which is placed the stub of a candle previously used at a wake. The witch buries this figure near the victim's house at night in order to cause his illness.

Improper diet or regimen can cause a great variety of illnesses, and diet is considered so important to well-being that those barrio people who consult the town doctor usually ask him to prescribe a special diet for the patient in addition to the medication he suggests. Proper diet is defined in terms of a complex of ideas that attributes hotness or coldness to foods. These attributes do not seem to be consistently related to the actual temperature of the material. For example, meat, fat, chocolate, and mangos are hot foods, while water is cold, and *papauza*, dry toasted tortilla, and aguardiente are apparently neutral or "refreshing." Neither the hot nor the cold condition is good or bad in itself. Rather, good health depends on equilibrium between the internal condition of the individual and the condition of things which affect him. Illness may result from adding hot to hot or cold to cold; taking a warm bath in hot weather or a cold bath in cold weather may produce headache and fever. Similarly, it may follow an excess of hot foods; it is said that people in Copala, who eat "nothing but mangos," suffer greatly from diarrhea. Illness may also come as a result of mixing hot and cold in a particular way; one can develop pains in the arms after grinding chocolate if one washes in water. Anger is especially likely to cause illness if one eats hot foods (pork, fat) while in the hot condition or if one bathes, turning one's hot condition suddenly to cold. As might be expected, the wrong type of food can also aggravate illness which already exists. It is bad for a sick person to drink either cold water or hot liquids; so he is given lukewarm water exclusively.

The hot-cold complex is important, then, not only in diagnosis but also in the treatment of illness. Avoidance of the type of food which caused the illness is one aspect of curing. Another is the administration of cooling or refreshing foods or herb baths, when the illness is regarded as a hot one. Diarrhea is treated by avoiding all hot foods and by eating refreshing or neutral fruits and dry tortillas. A person with a cold may be given a sponge bath in aguardiente mixed with mentholatum and camphor, or mentholatum and candle wax may be applied to his throat, temples, and the sides of his nose. Mejoral, a patent pain-killer, is considered refreshing and may be given in small quantities to children with colds. Fainting and nausea may be treated by application of a cooling herb, *ruda*, to the back of the neck and by drinking a mixture of lemon and bicarbonate of soda. Dizziness after an encounter with *mal aire* or the *tabayuku* is treated by blowing aguardiente from the mouth all over the patient's body and by applying a great number of herbs—*ruda* and myrrh and others. Anger-caused illness and illness due to fright are treated in much the same way. In the case of measles, several steps in the treatment participate in the hot-cold complex in different ways. First, a mixture of aguardiente and mexcal is blown over the patient's body to cool the skin and bring the rash to the surface. He is protected from wind, which might shock the body and drive the rash inward. (When the heat represented by the rash stays inside, the patient usually dies.) Then, some days after the rash has appeared, he is given a sweat bath. Barrio people explain that the heat of the sweat bath is a refreshing heat.

The sweat bath, which is used in combination with various herbs for fevers of other kinds and for rheumatism as well as for measles, is administered in a more or less permanent structure in the court-yard or house of the patient. Some barrio households have a *baño de refresco,* a sweat bath built of adobe, but most build a *baño de toro,* a temporary structure, when it is needed. The *baño de toro* is made by arching bamboo poles to form a framework some 6 feet long and 3 feet high. The framework is placed over a fireplace built with four adobes set in a square. A fire is built in the fireplace, and rocks the size of a softball are piled on top of it. The rocks are allowed to heat for several hours; in the meantime, small leafy branches (brought from the river) are tied together in bunches to form dusters. Finally, the framework is covered with several layers of mats, and the patient and his helper (a woman relative or a profession curer) go inside. Behind a blanket which covers the doorway to the bath, they undress. Water is thrown onto the rocks so that steam rises from them. Then the helper brushes the patient well with the bunch of branches for 20 minutes or more. On emerging from the bath, the patient wraps in a blanket and lies down. He should be given only warm water to drink, but he can have anything to eat that he wants. The sweat bath may be repeated several times at two-day intervals before the cure is considered complete.

In addition to herbs, patent medicines, and baths, a number of rituals are employed in curing illness. Illness caused by the evil eye is sometimes diagnosed by examining the inside of an egg for telling signs, and it can be cured only by the touch of the person who caused the contamination. In other types of illness in children, the patient may be taken to church for an *evangelio,* a short and simple service in which the priest reads scripture over the head of the child, and a candle is lighted. (Evangelio may also be read for children who are not ill as a prophylaxis.) There is some indication that the professional curers of the barrio use rituals or prayers in curing. It would be surprising if the belief in illness caused by fright (*espanto*) were not accompanied by some kind of ritual to retrieve the soul of the patient from the spot at which it was lost, for this combination of beliefs is common in Middle America and, indeed, occurs elsewhere in the Mixteca. Some curers are said to know how to suck foreign objects (inserted by witches) out of the patient's body. Divining the outcome of illness by means of an egg is also reported. The egg is rubbed on the afflicted part of the body and then stood on end. A small piece of incense is placed on top and lighted. If the heat of the burning incense breaks the egg, it is expected that the patient will die.

Ritual means are also taken to prevent illness. Babies often wear a pointed shell on a cord around their necks to prevent coughs. They can be protected from contamination caused by the presence of death and from spells cast by witches by a bag of selected herbs which the mother wears tied around her waist.

Curing may be attempted by members of the patient's immediate family, in the first instance. Herb remedies for simple illnesses are widely known, and aspirin is often bought in local stores. Often, also, the patient is given no medication at all but is allowed to rest and is given little food until the disease goes away of its own accord. Illness which is vague (e.g., headache, slight fever, listlessness) and not alarming in its symptoms may be tolerated by the patient and the family for days or even weeks. At some point, which differs in each household, the illness is defined as serious and treatment is begun. Home remedies and store-bought medicines are usually tried first, and it is when they have no effect that a professional curer is sought.

The barrio has several professional curers, all of them women who also serve as midwives. Their methods include the rituals described above, and it is they who apply the more elaborate herb baths required in cases of fright and anger. If the illness is judged to be caused by witchcraft, a witch from a neighboring community may be called in to cure it.

Local *curanderas* charge less and are generally more trusted than the town doctor, but barrio people occasionally consult the doctor. A resident doctor in Juxtlahuaca is a rarity, the only ones in recent years having been recent graduates doing their six months of required social service. To a considerable extent, they share the feeling of el Centro people toward the Indians and behave toward them in much the same way. Barrio people who visit the doctor are likely to be examined briefly or not at all and to be sold medication at greater than usual cost. Nevertheless, some families take their sick members there when the illness defies local treatment and they have the money. Frequently they ask for injections, one of the services that only the doctor can perform. While injections have the confidence of some barrio people, others fear them. It is rumored that the recent death of a barrio child was caused by one of the doctor's injections.

Praying to the saints may be an adjunct to any cure for an illness. An ill person may go to the church where the statues of the saints are kept and make a special prayer on an individual basis to the particular saint. The typical procedure would be for the individual to light a candle for the saint and to make an informal prayer to him. In a few cases, an individual would go to the priest and ask for a special mass or service. The practice of promising a saint a special mass if he will cure an illness is also known, although very rarely used. On the whole, the part played by the saints in curing is a nominal one and is primarily an adjunct to other methods.

Although illness is an everpresent concern in the barrio, it does not seem to be a dominant one. People make an effort to avoid illness by eating properly and behaving prudently (avoiding anger, aggression, and ritual contamination). When they become ill, they tend to wait patiently until they are well again. If the illness is severe or of long duration, they attempt to cure it—first by the means which are nearest at hand and least expensive, next by means which are thought more certain but also cost more, and, finally, by any means at all up to a given economic limit. Death, when it comes in spite of everything that has been done, is seen as a loss but also as an end to suffering, and it is accepted "if God wishes it."

※
※
※

Chapter 8

Funeral Ceremonies

A bell in the church is rung to signify that a death has taken place. This sounds different from the one signifying time for church; this one is rung a long time, very slowly. It is rung by male members of the deceased's family—sons, brothers, cousins, and so forth. When the men finish ringing the bell, they go out into the street and tell the people who has died. No special person is necessarily called to pronounce the death, in contrast to societies in which the padre or the eldest member of the family is expected to make this announcement. All the close family is gathered together immediately, including aunts, uncles, cousins, sons, daughters, father, mother, husband or wife, as well as particular compadres. They all sit with the body throughout the night, with candles burning. No special person is required to stay with the body, for instance, the mother or the husband, but all the members of the family who are able to come do so.

Women prepare the body of a woman for burial, while men prepare the body of a man. There is no bathing or washing of the body or combing of the hair. It is left just as it was when the person died except that new thick stockings and special death shoes made of palms, like huarches, are placed on the feet. If the deceased is a woman, her rebozo is placed around the head, covering her face and almost all of the body down to the feet. The arms and hands are folded over the chest. Dry cotton is placed in the nose and ears, but no other special preparations are used. A small white bag of heavy material is prepared, and inside it are placed two tablets of chocolate, ten cents worth of finely ground sugar in a separate bag, a tiny beater for mixing chocolate, two special, tiny, coarsely ground tortillas, two pieces of the meat that the family had for their last meal together, a bottle of water, and a spool of thread if it is a woman. If the person knew how to write, a pencil, small envelope, and paper are also placed inside the bag. This bag is supposedly laid over the shoulders, crossing under the chin and over the mouth. In addition, all the old clothes of the deceased are laid inside the coffin. If there is anything new that has not actually touched the body, it can be kept by the family, but all other clothing should be placed with the body. Serapes or blankets are not put in the coffin.

The corpse is laid in front of the family altar, where all the saints' pictures are placed together. There are many flowers gathered by the family and many that are later brought by the mourners. There are many candles—the small altar candles, the white candles used for light, and also the very tall, special fiesta candles, which are brown. These brown candles have all been blessed at the annual fiesta. The Indian incense, *copal,* is in its special dish in front of the body and is lighted as soon as death occurs. The body itself is placed on boxes to get it up off the floor until a casket can be prepared. A crucifix is not necessary on the family altar, but a special cross of vines is arranged on the dirt floor in front of the corpse. Palm mats are placed on the floor in front of the body for mourners to sit on. All the guests go first to the chief mourner, that is, the mother of a child or the husband or wife as the case may be, and to this person they give their gift of money. Most also bring candles or flowers or both. If a close friend or compadre is sick, he is not supposed to go to the wake, since there is bad air present, which makes it a dangerous place for a sick or weak person.

On entering the room of death, the mourner immediately goes to the altar, kneels in front of the chief picture or statue, and crosses himself. Then he lights the candle he has brought and places it somewhere on the floor near the corpse. Flowers are similarly placed nearby. Next the mourner retreats and sits on the floor on a mat. Praying is not obvious. The people merely sit and watch. They may talk quietly with one another. Drinks are served to the men, who may be off in one corner, and sometimes there is a great deal of joking and laughing. It is not necessarily a very solemn, quiet occasion.

The body must be interred before 24 hours have passed. If death occurs early in the day, the burial may take place the following morning; otherwise it always takes place late in the afternoon. It does not necessarily entail a visit to church nor is it necessary for a priest to officiate. He may come to the house if he is asked, but this involves a payment. Even if the priest does come to the house, he does not go with the body to the cemetery. However, even for the poorest, a song or prayer is said, and often musicians are invited to the house to play the music. A body must be buried during the daytime, never after sundown.

Food is served to all persons attending the wake. The type of food varies according to the amount of money in the family, on how much time there is in which to prepare it, and how much help is available. It can be anything from a simple repast of chocolate and bread to a complete meal with chile and turkey or beef. Food is served until time for the funeral procession to start, at which time the church bell is rung again to signify that it is time for the people to gather. All who care to may walk with the body up to the cemetery. They follow it in two lines, the women on one side of the street, the men on the other. Everyone walking in a funeral procession, not including children, should carry a tall candle. If one does not bring his own, it is up to the house of the deceased to supply one.

Children attending a funeral may not enter the room in which the body is laid out, but all the household or patio is open to them; they are fed the same food as the parents, and they are allowed to run and play freely. However, few parents bring their children because there might be bad air. Many children seem to enjoy walking in funeral processions, and their parents often bring them to this part of the ceremony. A small boy usually walks first, carrying the incense; then come the four men carrying the coffin. It is interesting to note that in every funeral we saw, the family of the deceased, no matter how poor, had provided a coffin. There was a great deal of variation in its ornamentation. For the people walking in the procession it is not necessarily a solemn or very sad occasion. True, there is no singing or dancing, but neither is there any wailing or weeping or any noise except the talking of the people walking in the lines. No one supposedly weeps at a funeral except the mother and perhaps the husband or the wife. The other people merely come to show their respect, not to weep. In fact, it is often difficult, when entering a house, to tell from the outward signs of cooking and preparations whether it is a wedding or a funeral.

The body is taken to the cemetery, which has one section for the Indians and one for the townspeople. The Indians are all buried with a cement slab over the top of the grave. It does not stand upright as a tombstone but lies flat on the ground. Since the Indian section is a small part of the cemetery, the graves are very close together. In fact, skeleton parts are often found during the digging and are simply thrown out with the dirt; no one seems to think anything about it. There is no special blessing at the grave. The hole has been prepared earlier by men who went up in the morning to do their duty, armed with two bottles of aguardiente. Often they are the men who will also carry the corpse back to the cemetery, which is high up on a hill and quite a climb. These are male members of the deceased's family, and they are not paid in money but are merely given drinks and a meal.

The casket is lowered into the grave; all the flowers that have surrounded the body in the home are placed on top of the casket; and then the clods of dirt are thrown over the flowers. Many persons throw handfuls of dirt to start the covering. Thanks are given at the graveside to those who have helped in any way, including special thanks to the particular society that lends the sacred brown candles. These thanks are expressed by some male members of the deceased's family. After the thanks, most of the women leave the cemetery, not waiting to see the grave filled and the ground level again. (It is interesting to note that the mothers or particular mourners do not go to the cemetery. When we asked why the mother of one woman who had died did not come, we were told that she had cried so much she could not stand to walk in the hot air up to the cemetery with all that bad air.) During the burial people have been standing or sitting on the cement stones that are gravemarkers. They seem also to step from grave to grave, as they are going out from the cemetery, without any particular thought that they might be walking on corpses. As the sun goes down, the majority of the men come down from the cemetery, finishing up their refilled bottles of aguardiente, talking and laughing with their shovels over their shoulders.

There are then eight days of visiting with the family. On the evening of the eighth day, there are candles around the altar, and on the ninth day "the raising of the cross" occurs. A bell, the particular low-ringing death bell, is rung in the church late in the afternoon to signify that it is time to gather for this particular ceremony. All persons attending bring the usual candles and the pesos for the house of mourning. The house altar is fixed as usual with the pictures of saints, the tall brown candles, the many vases and cans of flowers on the table and on the floor surrounding it. On the floor in front of the saints' pictures there is a cross, about a foot high, made out of plant leaves which are very white on the ends and so waxey in appearance they seem to be made of porcelain. A close relative of the deceased keeps the cross after the ceremony. In front of the cross on the floor there is a wooden box with a cross drawn on it with powdered lime. The numbers one to five are marked in ink around it.

These numbers are used to designate the five padrinos of the cross. Each padrino, especially chosen for this occasion, brings a tray of flowers and a large, special glass with an altar candle in it. As each padrino enters, he kneels, crosses himself, and places his candle on one of the inked numbers. When all five padrinos have entered, the ceremony can begin. Until this time, a dish of corn is served to all who enter, although many only come as far as the gate, hand in a peso, and leave. But careful note is made of each arrival, the gifts of food are sent to all whether they came in or not. Special palm spoons are made with which to eat the special cold dish, *pesole*. It is the job of one of the older men of the family to sit in the sun and carve these hundred or so spoons.

The ceremony always occurs at night, and so one fire is built in the path before the doorway to the house and another in the inner courtyard before the room of mourning. These two fires are supposedly only for light to guide people's feet and not for any signficant reason. A large dish of pesole and also a small one of mole are set on boxes on each side of the cross.

When all the padrinos are in attendance, the singing can begin. It is led by a man, usually, who sings a verse, after which a woman attendant or young girl who knows the responses very well leads the audience loudly. Three times a long group of prayers are said with the man alone leading and the woman and the rest of the audience responding. As the prayers start, all the people kneel. Each group of prayers takes from 20 to 35 minutes; thus by the time the third series comes along, many of the people are very tired. Nevertheless, all of the women, with their rebozos wrapped around them and their eyes looking downward, kneel on the dirt floor or on palm mats. Many of the men, however, are only partially kneeling and many are almost asleep by 11:30. Very few children attend this ceremony, and those who are present sleep beside their mothers. At the end of each series of prayers there is a breathing spell for relaxation and resting the knees. Everyone sits back and talk starts immediately—gossip of the village and other notes of interest. Many of the men step outside to have a drink and a walk in the night air, but the women usually remain inside the room.

It is interesting to note that few of the mourners' family are present —the women, that is. They are all outside by the cook shack preparing a meal to be enjoyed when the prayers are finished. At the end of the third group of prayers, the leader goes up in front of the cross, which is flat on the ground and completely surrounded by flowers, usually in tin cans, takes a flower, and dips it in a small cup or dish of holy or blessed water. He kneels and sprinkles the cross with holy water from the flower. Then he puts his lips to the cross, gets to his feet, and walks to the side of the room. This same performance is then repeated, first, by all the men in the room. It is a very orderly procession. Each one steps up, kneels down, sprinkles the cross, kisses it, gets to his feet, and moves off. There is no obvious social prestige involved except that the men of the deceased's family go first. After that there is no seniority or status preference, just whoever happens to be sitting along the wall as each one takes his turn. When the men have finished, the majority of them leave the room, and then the women do the same thing, going up to kneel and kiss the cross. When everyone in the room who cares to has performed this little ceremony, two men of the deceased's family return, carefully pick up the cross and carry it out into the open air, and stand with it there for a few moments. Then they return and place the cross upright on the family altar. This concludes the raising of the cross, and the people start talking and laughing and joking.

The musicians come in, and pesole is served to everyone. By this time it is usually between 11 and 12 o'clock at night, but the people, even those who have been sleepy the hour before, become wide awake and laugh and joke as they eat. Then gifts of food are sent around early in the morning to all who did not attend but who sent their little gifts of money, as well as to comadres or compadres of the family to whom the family of the deceased owes gifts. Then, as people are leaving, gifts of candles to light the way may be given to those going home in the darkness, since few people have flashlights and none have Coleman lanterns. So it is, at midnight, little bands of people can be seen walking down the street together. They pause to talk, then separate, and then two candles or two lights go on down the street.

The death of a child is treated quite differently. Children who are young, 12 or under, who have not been through confession, are called angelitos, and these "little angels" go directly to heaven. There is no need for the nine days of prayer and the raising of the cross for these little children, for they become angels the moment they stop breathing. They are dressed in long white robes trimmed with the color of the particular saint of that month. For example, if a little girl dies during June, she is dressed in the colors of the Virgin Mary, for this is her month. If a little boy dies in May, he is dressed in red and white, the colors of Jesus, for May is his month. Also, if a very small child dies, he may be dressed in the particular color of his saint's day, always combined with the white and gold. The long white robe has a gold belt with little gold tinseled slippers. A crown is placed on the child's head and a flower in each hand. The flowers may be waxed or artificial, or they may be real flowers. Also, a canopy of gauze is usually raised over the head to make almost an altar of this little angel. The baby's eyes are not closed; they are staring straight ahead in order to see God immediately. Four candles are placed on the table beside the child at each corner—north, east, south, and west.

Part II

Child Training

✤
✤
✤
✤
✤
✤

Chapter 9

Introduction

People in the barrio divide life into more or less distinct stages. Individuals in each stage are thought to possess certain qualities and characteristics that set them apart from individuals in other stages of life. Practices and beliefs concerning the various behavior systems vary according to the stage of development of the child. There are ideas about the kinds of behavior that are appropriate for individuals in each stage as well as special privileges and responsibilities associated with increasing maturity. In this section, the socialization of the behavior systems will be described and discussed in the framework of the stages of life as seen by the people of Santo Domingo barrio.

The first stage is that of *infancy*. The Mixteco word used for infants means "in darkness" and implies that the infant has no "awareness." When speaking Spanish, Santo Domingans use the term "creature" in referring to infants. About the time the infant is weaned, at the age of 1 or 2 years, he gains "awareness" and enters the second stage, which is *early childhood*. The Mixteco word for this period means "this child now knows." Early childhood continues until the second set of teeth is replacing the milk teeth. This marks the beginning of *late childhood* and takes place in the sixth and seventh year. At this time the child begins to have the capacity to reason. The fourth stage, *youth,* begins when the child becomes actively aware of sex. In theory this begins at age 12. Until the age of 12, a child who dies is thought to become an angel; beyond that age he becomes responsible for his status in the next world.

Despite these ideas, the differences between late childhood and youth are much less marked than between the earlier stages of life. Full maturity or *adulthood* is reached with economic independence, which is generally associated with marriage. In talking with Santo Domingans, one always hears them say that adulthood begins with marriage. It happens that there are about a dozen men in their twenties or thirties in the barrio who have never been married. When asked whether he is adult or not, the Santo Domingan will say, "Yes," and then point out that he is economically independent, and this is what really distinguishes him from a youth. Sixteen is the age given to mark the beginning of adulthood.

The people agree that the stages outlined above are the ideal. They recognize, however, that in practice numerous factors can speed up or slow down development in any specific case and thus there is variation about the stated transition points. For example, the youngest child spends more time in early childhood than his older siblings. Or again, if a woman has two children close together, the older one is weaned earlier and thus enters early childhood sooner than otherwise.

With two rather dramatic exceptions, the transition between stages of life is gradual and continuous for the barrio child; one stage blends into another with no sudden shift in expectations, and what has gone before is consistent and preparatory for what follows. The two exceptions are: (1) the transition from infancy to early childhood, marked by abrupt weaning and a shift from sleeping with parents to sleeping alone or with siblings, and (2) the transition from early childhood to late childhood, marked by a change in the amount of succorance allowed and nurturance given the child, together with increased expectations in responsibility, self-reliance, and obedience, all backed up by a shift in techniques of discipline.

The infant up to the age of 2 differs from an adult in two respects besides those that are apparent in size and knowledge. Infants are thought of being, along with other animals, without awareness and the ability to reason. It is thought that no learning takes place until the infant develops awareness. Awareness grows and increases slowly and naturally without human help or interference, beginning at the end of the first year of life and continuing until it is fully developed at the age of 2. The ability to reason does not develop until the age of 7. Like awareness, reason matures without human intervention. Near the end of the sixth year, a child will begin to show evidences of reason, and by the age of 8 it will be a fully developed characteristic. Since the ability to understand and learn behavior appropriate to adulthood depends on the ability to reason, children younger than 6 are not expected to begin to behave like adults, and their behavior cannot be judged as morally good or bad.

Every individual gains awareness and reason much as he cuts teeth or matures physically. It is recognized that some may develop these qualities at an earlier or later age than others, but every individual, in the natural course of events, will mature in these respects just as surely as in physiological traits. Since every adult has these abilities, they cannot account for observed differences between individuals.

"Every person has his own character. Some people are happy, some are mean," say the Santo Domingans. Such differences are believed to arise through two kinds of factors: inheritance and learning. A child inherits its personal characteristics through the blood. Even though rearing and learning do and can affect these characteristics, a person never loses his blood, and eventually it will come out. For example, if one has a bad temper, it can be explained in terms of the father or mother or some relative having had bad temper. Characteristics inherited in the blood may lie dormant for many years before showing up in behavior. It is common for some inherited characteristics to first show up at marriage, for example, jealousy in women.

One inherits blood from both the mother and the father, and most characteristics would come from them, although on occasion one might get the blood of a more distant relative, such as an uncle or aunt or grandparent. One inherits more from the father or mother, depending upon which one is the most dominant and energetic. One of the values held very highly by the barrio people is that a husband and wife should be about equal in dominance and energy, and it is believed that inheritance of blood is usually equal from each parent. Where differences were said to occur, however, it was more commonly found that women were thought to be more energetic and dominant than their husbands rather than the reverse. Corresponding to this belief is the idea that the mother's blood is stronger in more children than the father's blood.

Differences in siblings are thought to arise because not all children of the same parents get the same blood. Even if they get blood in the same proportion from each parent, the children will come out differently because, "Some of them get the blood of a parent and some of them get the dominant blood from an aunt, an uncle, or other relative," says a Santo Domingan.

The way in which inheritance and learning are related in the development of an individual is very neatly summed up by Juan Chorra, one of our informants. "One's character comes from the blood, but what one learns is very important. One learns until these things that one learns become a habit. Habits are very hard to get rid of."

Parents are responsible for the training of their children. They are believed capable of shaping the development of the child and are expected by the community to do the best they can. If, despite everything a parent can do, the child does not turn out well because of bad blood somewhere else in the family, the parent is not held responsible. On the other hand, if the parent does not give the child adequate training and the child turns out to be bad, then the parent is felt to be responsible. The beliefs are sufficiently flexible to allow the Santo Domingans to shift blame according to their attitudes toward the parents. When asked why specific people turned out as they did, the choice of explanations seemed to depend on the following variables: how well the parent is liked, the standing of the family in the community, the number of bad relatives, the degree of resemblance between parents and child in other respects, and so on.

Personality is most maleable between the ages of 6 or 7 and 12. Before the age of 6, the child is not thought to possess sufficient reasoning power to really learn effectively. After 12, it becomes increasingly difficult to change the basic character of a person until he reaches adulthood at about 18, when it becomes impossible to alter his character. At this age, the results of earlier learning and training are fixed; the final effects of blood show themselves, and one's character is fixed for life. The good parent is the one who feels responsible for his children until they marry. If the community consensus is that a parent has done his duty for his children, he is not judged responsible for his children after marriage.

The above sketch presents an idealized version of the barrio theory of development. There is great variation in the way in which this ideal is translated into practice. The following chapters will trace the process of socialization in some detail and introduce observational and interview data.

⚘

⚘

⚘

Chapter 10

Pregnancy and Childbirth

To bear many children is viewed by barrio women as a desirable and natural part of life. The ideal is to have many children of both sexes while still young, since children are viewed as a natural part of life and as economic assets, especially as providers for old age. If there are several children, the burden will not be too great for any one of them.

The beliefs about children as a natural part of life are summed up in the phrase, "Children come as the rain." The rain comes in season; there may be periods of drought, but it always comes. Without rain to support the crops, the barrio could not exist. So it is with children. They come one after another, with shorter or longer periods between. But without children, the barrio could not go on.

Economically children contribute much to the family. At cooperative works in the barrio, each family is expected to contribute its share of labor, both male and female. Families who do not have sufficient children to fulfill these obligations would be expected to hire outside help or call on other relatives. Either of these would involve extra burden, for calling on other relatives would obligate one to repay in kind later. Also, within the family itself, children begin early to help their parents; girls help their mothers with younger children and in household tasks, while boys help their fathers in the fields and with the animals and other male tasks. Thus, while on the whole there is little over-all preference for a child of one sex over the other, a father prefers sons who will help him, a mother prefers daughters who will help her.

Families who have only children of one sex receive the sympathy of the other barrio members. Chencho Chorra and his wife had three boys and a girl, for example. When the little girl died, Chencho and his wife showed more grief than was usual at the death of a child, and the barrio was very sympathetic and said, "The poor woman, now she has no one to help her." Salazar, on the other hand, has four girls and no boys. Everyone feels that it is a shame that he has no one to help him with his work. On occasions when he has to call on relatives to help him with his share of a cooperative work party, the men say, "It's too bad you don't have any boys to help out."

The birth of a healthy, well-formed child is always an occasion for rejoicing. Of all the fiestas, the one given soon after a child is born, when he is baptized, is most joyous.

Traditionally, and still to a considerable degree, a couple without children is not considered married. It is only with the appearance of the first child that the woman is said to have demonstrated her womanhood, and the couple becomes a family. There is one couple in the barrio who have lived together for several years but have no children. Everyone feels very sorry for them, and they express great desire for children. Some people explain it by saying they were too old when they were married, while others say that they are being punished for something they have done in the past. Their situation is viewed by themselves and others as unnatural, and they do not enter into full participation of the barrio social life as a consequence.

Several kinds of preparations are used to induce pregnancy. A common one is made from fresh pine resin which is boiled with three roots from a corn plant and taken hot. Another preparation is a brew made from a sage plant.

Women who want to control the number of children they have are viewed with considerable disapproval. They have techniques which they believe will control conception as well as cause abortion. They believe that drinking water in which a metal worker has washed his metal tools when they were hot will prevent conception, but this is thought to be both bad and dangerous since it not only prevents pregnancy but also causes sickness. When the weather gets cold, the woman's feet will swell, and when the moon comes out, her belly will be painful. Abortion can be produced by taking the squeezings of a dozen cold lemons. These practices are highly disapproved of in the barrio and are attributed mainly to townspeople.

Infanticide, or the killing of newborn infants, is only practiced when a child is born "with the face of an animal." Children who are deformed in other ways are reared much like normal children.

Conception is known to result from sexual intercourse. Children learn this at an early age by asking questions about cattle that are brought together for breeding purposes. There is little secrecy about the matter although there may be some jesting by the men.

A woman knows she is pregnant when "her moon disappears," that is, when menstruation stops. The first person she notifies is her mother or her mother-in-law if she lives in the latter's courtyard. They are in charge of advising the husband and the fathers of both the husband and wife. The woman is embarrassed if others are told, especially if it is her first pregnancy. The rest of the family become aware only when her belly begins to swell. There is modesty, though no secrecy, about later stages of pregnancy.

If a pregnant woman feels like eating something on a whim, it should be satisfied lest she suffer a miscarriage or a premature birth. It is part of a husband's duty to provide his wife with the foods she desires, and there are no restrictions as to what she may eat. However, it is believed that eating too much causes painful childbirth.

There are no special taboos on a pregnant woman's activities during pregnancy. She continues to grind for tortillas, wash clothes, and engage in other normal work. The only precaution mentioned is that she should not carry heavy objects. A couple may continue to have sexual intercourse up to the time of birth. No special positions are used for the protection of the fetus.

Nausea during pregnancy is not unusual during the first three months. It is thought to be a natural condition of pregnancy for certain women, not a reflection of character and not related to other qualities she might have.

When a woman feels that the baby is going to arrive before it is due, she takes steps to prevent the miscarriage or premature birth by drinking a concoction brewed from the leaves of *Santa Maria,* a species of *artemisa,* and other herbs. This is supposed to "fix" the fetus so that it sticks better inside and does not "fall out early." The two major causes of miscarriage are thought to be the frustration of some food craving of the mother and lifting heavy objects. Premature babies, when they survive, are given no special or differential treatment, nor are there any special beliefs about them.

About a month before the baby is expected, special treatments are supposed not only to keep the fetus in the proper position for birth but also to loosen the fetus gradually so that birth will be less painful. A midwife massages the hips and stomach gently with warm oil of almonds.* The massages are sometimes done by hand, and sometimes,

---

* In other areas of Mexico, the massages are sometimes very vigorous, and in Tzintzuntzan, Foster attributes many miscarriages to the heavy massaging.

after being rubbed with oil, a rebozo is used. The rebozo is pulled back and forth around the woman's stomach. The midwife also puts catalan in her mouth and blows it on the buttocks and hips of the pregnant woman. This also is thought to help loosen the child and make childbirth less painful. These treatments are given about once a week during the last month of pregnancy.

There are many beliefs current among barrio people about the effects of the experiences and behavior of pregnant women on their children. If a pregnant woman sees the eclipse of the moon, the baby will "lose moisture" and will be born with defects caused by the lack of moisture. Harelips and defective extremities are most commonly given as examples of such defects. A pregnant woman should be especially careful about how she speaks of others. Bad gossip about others or direct aggressive statements can affect her unborn child. For example, if she said to another person, "You have the face of a fox (or other animal)," her child might be born with such a face. Although some recognize a hereditary factor, it is a common belief that twins are caused by a woman eating double or twinned fruit, especially a double banana. Not all women admit to this belief, and some skeptics tend to joke about it. On one occasion we happened to run across a double banana and offered it along with some single bananas to several women. Although they laughed and joked, none of them would take it. The twinned fruit does not need to be eaten during pregnancy to produce twins, and even young girls avoid it. Twins are not feared, but neither are they desired since they are thought to be more trouble than other children.

Not all defects of infants are thought to arise from the experiences or actions of the mother during pregnancy. Some arise by chance or providence. Mothers also expressed the belief that the unborn child might be deformed "just because he wants to." The beliefs of the people in the effects of the experiences and actions of the pregnant woman are strong enough, however, so that in no case did we observe practices contrary to the beliefs.

The course of the first pregnancy is very similar to that of subsequent ones although women seem more fearful after their first delivery. There is some difference in the husband's and wife's attitudes toward pregnancy. Women's attitudes vary from a somewhat fatalistic acceptance to pleasant anticipation. The men exhibit more anticipation and generally prefer larger families than their wives. The women would be content with an average of four children, while the men would prefer about six. Due to the high rate of infant mortality, most couples never have more than four to six surviving children.

These differences in the attitudes of the husband and wife are related to several factors. Girls tend to marry younger than men because, according to Mexican law, marriage cannot take place before compulsory military service. Although this law is sometimes circumvented, men are generally over 20 at marriage, while a girl would be considered undesirable if not married by that age. Becoming a mother raises the status of a woman somewhat, but the improvement in status is much greater for a man. When he becomes a father, he moves from youth to manhood and acquires a new independence.

Ideally a man will be more affectionate and thoughtful of his wife's needs during her pregnancy. This ideal is generally reflected in practice for the first child or two, but after this time there is no observable difference in a husband's behavior during the pregnancy of his wife.

When a woman is ready to give birth to a child, a warm vapor, like steam or smoke, appears where the infant's head is to appear. With the appearance of this vapor and the commencement of pains, the midwife, the mother, the mother-in-law, a compadre or two, the husband, and any others who might come to help, are sent for. The birth takes place in the house of the couple having the child, and the people who are to aid, along with the girl's father, assemble there. No children or other men should be present.

The woman kneels with her knees well separated on a woven straw mat which has been laid on the dirt floor for the purpose. To help her make sufficient exertion, she is given two raw eggs to eat. These are broken directly into her mouth by the midwife or one of the other women present. When the pain begins, she is given a bitter tea made from *artemisa,* which is supposed to help expel the child. If the woman tires from holding her posture too long, she may get up and walk around. The women present also rub her belly with almond oil.

When the child begins to emerge, the midwife places herself in front of the mother to receive the child, while the husband, or sometimes another woman, holds the mother down strongly by the waist. At this point, a wide sash is adjusted around the woman's waist. The husband assists until the infant is born and until the sash is adjusted. If the sash is not put on tightly and adjusted properly, the woman could get sick and die, since it is thought to prevent the blood and the placenta from rising and is said to help expel the placenta more rapidly.

The mother must continue to exert herself to expel the placenta. She does this by blowing in a bottle and by chewing a few leaves of *yerba buena,* mint with salt, to help in her exertion. Sometimes her throat is tickled with a feather or finger to cause nausea in order to aid the expulsion of the placenta. After the placenta has been discharged, it is placed in a rag and rolled up in the straw mat and placed in a tree so that the child, when he grows up, will be able to climb trees. The placenta should be very clean because if any dirt gets on it, it may affect the eyes of the child. Once the afterbirth is expelled, the mother changes her clothes but does not bathe or touch water. If pain continues after birth, the mother takes a special tea brewed without sugar.

In case of delayed births, the mother lies down on the mat and a rebozo is put around her waist. The two ends of the rebozo are held by the midwife and moved first toward one side and then to the other, sliding over the body with steady pressure in a rotary movement. No one knows why births are delayed. Some attribute it to God's will.

If the child is in an improper position for birth, the midwife corrects it by external pressure and massage. In no case does the midwife put her hand inside the mother. If the child begins to be born hand first, a needle is used to prick the little hand so that it will pull back inside and the mother is placed almost on her head with her legs upward. The midwife then blows on her so that the baby will straighten out.

When the baby is born, if he doesn't want to cry, the midwife blows a little warm alcohol near his heart. The baby is immediately placed on a new straw mat with a clean cloth. His umbilicus is tied with a thread and is cut above the tie with scissors which have been heated with a candle made of grease. After the cord is cut, the exposed end is burned with a candle. The cord is then passed through several squares of cloth previously prepared for the purpose with center holes. Grease is rubbed on the cord and the squares of cloth. The body of the child is then greased with almond oil, and it is dressed in a tiny shirt. The baby is given a spoonful of oil. This is said to clean out his stomach. The infant is then given to his mother, and they lie down together.

During the first two days, the infant is fed by some woman other than the mother. Any woman who is currently nursing her child may offer her services. The mother squeezes the colostrum from her breasts during this period unless there are no other women available in which case, the infant is given a little tea and the mother gives him the breast the second day. To encourage the flow of milk, a green herb spice is toasted and ground into a paste for the mother. The paste is rubbed on the back between the mother's shoulders and on her hips and around her breasts.

Grease is rubbed on the umbilical cord until it falls off. When it falls off, it is kept wrapped in a little rag and used in the preparation of an eye wash used in the treatment of children's eye diseases. The cord of a male child is used to treat a female child and vice versa. Once the umbilicus has fallen off, the child is bathed in lukewarm water and rubbed with almond oil.

After birth, the mother is supposed to rest in bed 40 days. She sleeps alone with the infant in her arms and does not resume her sexual life for two months. In practice, she may get up a little before this but almost always confines herself to the inside of the house and never does any hard work. She must not touch a needle, hold a broom, or do any lifting. When she does begin to get up, she does it very gradually. Women may visit her, bringing bread, chocolate, a peso for clothes for the child, or some other small gift. They do not look at the infant, for if something happened to him, they might be accused of "evil eye." During the first few days the mother can only drink chocolate and broth and eat meat of chicken or a crisp, toasted tortilla of a special type. She cannot eat chile, greases, pork, black or green beans, or any "cold" foods. She can drink atole, white broth, warm tea, and should neither touch nor drink cold water.

Two or three days after birth, an herbal brew is prepared for the mother. She washes herself with this mixture and then goes back to bed. Six days after birth, the mother is given her first sweat bath. Before entering the bath she loosens her hair and rubs her head with "a good piece of Juxtlahuacan leather." She can only wash her hair during the 40 days. If she were to cut it on any account, it could "go inside" and death could result. In the sweat bath she is assisted by two female relatives. Her head is washed twice and then her body is bathed. She must take between 12 and 15 of these sweat baths before she is considered recovered.

We have almost no reports of women dying in childbirth, and childbirth is not considered dangerous for the mother. The case is very different for the infant. During the year of the study several infants died immediately or soon after birth, and an analysis of the genealogical material confirms the high rate of infant mortality. The average woman in the barrio has borne twice as many children as are surviving. Not all of these children have died right after birth. The period around weaning, as reported later, is also very hazardous. The figures cannot be taken as too accurate, but 20% mortality due to advanced miscarriage, premature births resulting in death, and infant deaths, is a conservative estimate. When an infant is born prematurely and dies, he is buried in the cemetery as is a fetus that is born dead or dies at birth.

Chapter 11

Infancy

After birth, the infant is wrapped in soft, usually old, clothes and held in the arms of the mother. For the first eight days he is close to his mother continuously, either in her arms while sleeping or being rocked during the day. After this time the infant may be put in a small, shallow, wooden cradle which hangs from the ceiling by ropes. There he sleeps for short periods during the day.

The first few weeks of life are considered very dangerous for the new baby, who is thought to have little resistance. There is much reality to this belief, for he is susceptible to diarrhea, parasites, and other ever-present ailments. Infants, particularly under the age of 2 or 3 months, are especially prone to the effects of "evil eye" and witches. This is one of the reasons given for confining the mother and child to the house for the first 40 days. As mentioned in an earlier chapter, an infant is not exposed to the dead at funerals.

The first 8 to 15 days, while the mother stays in bed, and the remaining time of the 40 when she sits around the house without doing very much work, no one but the family is supposed to see the baby lest he become sick and die. A sleeping baby is particularly vulnerable, since he is unconscious and cannot protect himself. This is one of the reasons a rebozo, or cloth, is always kept over the face of younger infants. Older infants are covered while sleeping, partly to ward off flies and partly to protect them from "evil eye."

"Evil eye" may be caused unwittingly by a relative, friend, or stranger who covets the child and stares at him directly. It may be caused willfully by a witch. The most common symptoms are vomiting and fever. It may be cured by the guilty person touching the victim if the act is unintentional. Two examples from our case histories of "evil eye" will help to illustrate the concept further.

The first example concerns unintentional effects of staring. Reina, a young girl of 13, attended a fiesta with her parents. An older woman looked at Reina several times during the evening because "she liked Reina." The next day Reina became ill with a fever and vomiting. Several remedies were tried without effect. Finally, the older woman was called; she came and touched Reina, and then the illness went away.

The second example concerns intentional effects of "evil eye." A couple in the barrio had no children and were very sad because they could have none. A young unmarried girl had an infant daughter, and her mother suggested that she give it to the childless couple. She did so, and the couple was very happy. When the baby was 3 months old, an old lady reputed to be a witch from Santa Rosa (a small village about 2 miles south of the barrio) came by one day and looked at the infant. The next day the baby came down with a high fever. She had this fever for 20 days, and nothing seemed to help her. A *curandera* (a woman who cures illness) was called in and tried everything she knew of to cure the baby. One day the infant rallied slightly and opened her eyes. That night, at midnight, the mother heard a knock at the door. When she opened it, she saw no one. On re-entering the room she saw a large, black cat walking around the mat on which the child was sleeping. She tried to hit the cat with a stick, but the stick "went through the cat" and she could not get it away. Then suddenly the cat disappeared. At three the next afternoon, the child died.

In talking with several people about this case, the following beliefs were brought out. Everyone agreed that the infant died from "evil eye." The witch was said to have a "strong" eye. Some of the people thought that the cat had been sent by the witch, while others said that it was just unfortunate that such an evil animal came when the child was already so ill that she had no defense against it.

Infants must be protected from the effects of witches. Informants said there were no witches in the barrio but named one woman in the central part of town and one woman in Santa Rosa. More distant towns were said to have many witches. The witch in town is said to attack only children under 3 to 4 months of age. When asked how they knew the woman was a witch, people say, "She goes out every night, and no one sees her going or coming." The following episode is attributed to the work of the witch in towns.

A mother awoke one night to find her infant daughter gone from her side. The mother jumped up from her bed and hurried to the door, calling the infant's name. She found her child on the step crying hard. The baby had blood beneath both ears and under her chin. No one was visible in the street in any direction. The mother comforted the infant; and the next day, she called in a curandera. The curandera cured the child and there was no lasting ill effect.

There are various ritual precautions that may be taken to ward off "evil eye," witches, and other evil influences. The mother frequently puts scissors, or even crossed sticks, at the head or the foot of the crib to cut any evil powers. Small nuts, not carved in any special way, are prepared by boring a hole through them so that they may be tied to a string which is put around a new baby's wrist to ward off evil.

To protect infants from "evil air," small caps are put on their heads. Since there is, in fact, a great deal of wind and many drafts which enter through the thatched or roughly tiled roofs, this precaution serves practical, as well as ritual, purposes.

Not all illness in infants is attributed to witches and "evil eye." We have records of five infants who died from measles during the period of the study. The disease was not thought to be caused by any outside agent, and deaths resulting from it were treated as due to natural causes. Death is said to result when "the measles don't come out, but turn inward and cause death."

Young infants are rarely taken out of the house and, in theory, should not leave the house for 40 days after birth except to be baptized. The mother is constantly close to the child. In practice, the 40 days' rest for the new mother is not strictly followed. Because of the press of work and other factors, the women will occasionally enter the courtyard; near the end of the 40 days they may even walk to the market or to the house of a relative. On these occasions the infant is carried in the mother's rebozo, but no part of the infant is ever exposed to air or to sight. For the first year the infant is carried in a prone position. It would be considered very bad manners for anyone to show any curiosity about seeing the infant. After a year the child may sit in the rebozo swing.

Mothers do not burp their new infants over the shoulder until they are about 4 months old, since it is thought dangerous to hold the child up over the shoulder before he can hold up his own head. They say that a new infant is "like a tender flower—you would break the stem." The backbone of the new infant is also considered to be very weak, and one has to handle the infant very carefully to avoid injuring it.

The responsibility for the care of an infant falls primarily to the mother, especially during the first four or five months. In the interviews, we asked the mothers who had spent the most time with their children when they were infants. Three fourths of the mothers responded that they had. Older sisters and grandmothers account equally for the remaining quarter of the cases. We also asked mothers who would take care of the child in case the mother was busy. One third of the mothers responded that they themselves would work with the children on their backs, while the other two thirds indicated that someone else would take care of their infants. The people mentioned, in order of frequency, were as follows: sisters, grandmother, and then aunt. All but 20% of the mothers indicated that someone other than themselves took care of the infant at least part of the time.

In general, our observations indicated that the mother is almost the exclusive caretaker during the first 40 days. After that time, the extent to which other older females participate is highly related to their availability. If there are older sisters in the household, they invariably take over a large share of the caretaking after the first two months. If there are no older sisters, then the grandmother or aunt will take over this function, if such a person happens to live in the compound or is close by. The empirical rule seems to be that the mother has the primary responsibility, but if the household is such that an older female is available to share in this task, she is pressed into service by the mother when she is busy or when she leaves the household for marketing or to wash clothes. In one family where there were only older brothers in the household, they sometimes took over the caretaking duties. This was commented on in the barrio and was thought to be an undesirable state of affairs.

Slightly less than half the mothers indicated that persons other than themselves had nursed their infant child. Most frequently mentioned was the aunt of the child; one grandmother was mentioned. In every case but one, however, the substitute was a close relative.

The other half indicated that no other woman had nursed their children but explained that this was because there were no other women in the extended family capable of nursing the child.

When a substitute nurse is used, it is most frequently during a short period when the mother is absent from the household and does not take the infant, as, for example, a trip to the market or to the stream for bathing or washing clothes. Actually, in these cases the mother most frequently takes a nursing child along with her, and it is only during the transition stage to early childhood that she might leave the child at home. Generally, when the mother is present, there is no substitution. Rather, one of the other women in the household might temporarily take over some of the grinding duties and other work of the mother. It is not at all uncommon for a mother to carry on simple tasks like shelling corn while she is nursing, nor is it uncommon to see mothers nursing their children in the market while carrying on trading activities there. The following exerpt from an interview gives an example of one mother's attitude toward substitute nurses.

Q. When he was still nursing, at times you allowed someone else to give him the breast? Did you not? That is, someone else like a sister or female friend?

A. Yes. Josefa gave him her breast because sometimes I would leave him sleeping and I went out, and if he woke, she would nurse him.

Q. In what situation did you allow Josefa to breast feed Abel?

A. Only when I was not there. If I was there, even if I was busy, I gave him the breast. Because if some other woman nurses them, it can do harm. I ate nothing fresh, no pineapple, coconut nor avocado nor banana or another kind of banana. Other women do eat these things but I do not. I took care of my milk so that it would not be harmful to the child. Some children get diarrhea and die if they take milk from other women than their mother.

Q. Was Abel allowed to breast feed whenever he asked?

A. Yes. She (referring to Josefa) gave it to him because she was there, and I had to go to the market almost every day. Abel's reddish hair he got from his mother, Josefa, because she nursed him a bit, so that she who gave him her breast is also his mother and he calls her mother. I tell him to call her mother so that he will love her more. (Note: Josefa is an aunt by marriage of Abel. Abel's mother's belief here that the child can inherit characteristics of the woman who nurses him, through her milk, is a distinct one, and no other mother mentioned this belief.)

Although fathers are generally affectionate toward their infant children, it is not thought to be their duty or responsibility to care for them. The father actually spends only a small part of the daylight hours in the household, for he is generally out in the fields. In the evening, or early in the morning, the father may pick up his infant child and jounce him on his knee for a short period, but if the child is wet or cries, the mother, sister, or grandmother will immediately take the responsibility of attending to the infant's needs. In the interviews, no mother reported that her husband aided in the care of the infant. Most reported that at night or during siestas or early in the morning, the husband might hold the baby for a moment or two, but nothing more.

Babies spend a great deal of time in their mothers' arms, and they are generally offered the breast at every little cry. They are rocked and go to sleep with the breast in their mouths, which thus serves as a pacifier. After the initial 40-day period, they sleep with both the mother and father.

Babies are never laid on the floor or placed on mats until they are a year old. During the day they sleep in a wooden box or cradle with a palm mat on the bottom and a rebozo over their head. The cradle hangs by a rope from the ceiling in the main room of the house. It is swung back and forth periodically by the mother or other close female relative. An infant is held and rocked in arms to put him to sleep before he is placed in the cradle. An infant who wakes up and cries will immediately be taken from the cradle and held by some older female caretaker. Once he is old enough to be placed on the floor, his movements are unrestricted as long as he stays on the mat.

Small babies are kept rather clean and changed fairly often. They are bathed and rubbed with oil the first few days of life and later are wiped with water and a clean rag; generally no soap is used. The bath water is placed in the wooden tub, which is put out in the yard to be warmed by the sun. Water brought directly from the well or the river is not used, for it is considered to be too cold. Babies are not actually put into the bath bowl; rather, they are sponged off. Small children beyond infancy may be placed in the wooden bath bowl.

Infants are dressed in a cotton shirt with diapers made of rags or cloth. These are tied on with a separate length of material, not pinned as is our custom generally. The baby is wrapped in a square piece of wide cloth. In poorer families this may be an old rebozo; in others, soft cotton material is used. The blanket is wrapped lightly, not tightly, from the arm pits down. This restricts movement somewhat but not completely. Infants at this age are generally very quiet and do not exhibit much physical movement. For about 10 months they are swaddled in this way most of the day and always at night.

Older children, from about 6 to 12 months, are generally changed less frequently than small babies. After a baby learns to walk, he will frequently be seen in the courtyard without any clothes other than a ragged shirt, but no attempts are made to toilet train the infant.

Girls' ears are generally pierced the first week or so. No special ceremony is performed. A small hole is pierced with a needle or pin by the mother or aunt, and a thread is drawn through the hole and tied in a little loop. The thread is merely to keep the hole open until the child may begin to use earrings—usually in late childhood and then only on special occasions.

An idea of the general behavior of the mother with respect to an infant is probably most easily communicated by excerpts from an actual observation. The following observation was taken of a mother with her 1-year-old boy. The setting is inside a cook shack where the mother and several other women are engaged in cleaning up after a meal at a fiesta.

The mother has one arm around the child, and he is standing and moving around her, holding on tightly to her all the time. The mother talks and smiles at him and wipes his face with her hand. He begins to cry, and the breast is immediately offered; he nurses for about a minute and a half and then stands up, holding onto the mother's arm and drops her breast. He makes many goo-ing sounds, and the mother answers in "cuddly tones." He cries again, and the mother holds his face and looks into his eyes, then the child reaches inside her dress for the breast and pulls it out. The mother unsnaps the blouse, and the child stands on her knee to nurse, the mother continuing to dry the dishes. He nurses for two minutes and then drops the breast again. The mother refastens her dress and continues work, talking to the women around her. The child stands on her legs as she is kneeling and he pulls at her earrings and her hair. The mother does not appear to notice this. The child cries again, and the breast is offered again, for the third time in ten minutes. He nurses two sucks and pushes it away. The mother refastens her dress and shows no annoyance. The child cries a little, and the mother looks around and gets a tortilla and breaks off a small piece and gives it to him. The child takes it and starts sucking on it and is quiet.

✸

✸

✸

Chapter 12

Early Childhood

The transition from infancy to early childhood is marked by several changes in the treatment of the child, the most important of which are weaning and a change in sleeping arrangements. During infancy the child sleeps in the same bed with his parents or, more rarely, in a cradle next to his parents' bed. At the transition into early childhood the child begins sleeping with his siblings rather than his parents. Thus children in both early and late childhood sleep together. The third important change is that the care of the infant, which has been primarily in the hands of the mother, is transferred to older siblings or cousins.

The parents' conception of the nature of the child at this stage differs in some important respects from the concept of the child as an infant. One of the more important of these ideas is the belief that the child develops or gains "awareness" on entering early childhood. The child is conceived of as being aware of himself as a distinct entity as well as developing awareness of other human beings as individuals. A child of this age, however, is not thought of as having developed the capacity for reason. In Mixtec belief, the child in this early stage is capable of learning by sheer repetition but is not thought of as having the capacity to learn by reason; nor can a child of this age recognize right from wrong, and he is not expected to be responsible for his behavior.

One of the more interesting ways in which this belief is related to the attitudes and behavior of the adults and older children toward a child is in the amount of nurturance given to children in this stage. For example, when a young child falls or hurts himself by any means, he is immediately nurtured and given comfort by an older sibling or cousin and is never ridiculed for the behavior because it is taken for granted that he does not know any better. As we shall see in the next chapter on late childhood, this attitude undergoes great change, for then the child is conceived of as having the ability to reason and to distinguish right from wrong. In that stage he would be ridiculed rather than comforted in such a situation.

Relatively little distinction is made between the treatment given to boys and that given to girls at this stage of life. Both boys and girls are carried around a great deal by the older children, and there is no distinction made on the basis of sex in the amount of nurturance and attention received from the older caretakers. The relatively simple tasks required of children are undifferentiated with respect to the sex of the child. The young child is not seen as making any contributions to the labor supply of the family; rather, this period is one in which the child is learning some simple skills by imitation and demonstration.

Weaning generally takes place at the age of 1 or 2 years. Ninety per cent of the mothers reported that they had weaned their children by the age of 2. Those who nursed longer than two years mentioned that there were no younger children and that this accounted for their nursing the child to the age of $2\frac{1}{2}$. Nursing may continue well into pregnancy. Almost all mothers, however, stop nursing during the fifth or sixth month of a new pregnancy. Some reported that the milk was not "good" beyond this time, that it would turn sour and might make the nursing child sick. Another frequently mentioned reason for weaning at this time was the amount of energy and strength available to the mother, the feeling being that it was just too difficult physically to carry a baby of some size and still continue to nurse.

The most striking uniformity of weaning is the abruptness with which it takes place. Weaning was abrupt in all but one case of the 22 mothers intensively studied. Half of the mothers used a bitter herb or dirt on the breast to discourage nursing. The herbs mentioned included saliva and *yerba maestra*. Just over a third of the mothers reported that they used the technique of leaving the child with a relative for a couple of days. Thus we see that although there is variation in the time of weaning and in the techniques used, there is almost complete uniformity in the abruptness with which weaning takes place. After weaning, when the baby cries, he is frequently given a liquid, such as coffee or milk, as a substitute for the mother's breast. This is one of the very few uses of milk in the barrio, for it is considered an expensive luxury under normal circumstances. Also, during the day the child may be given bits of food, such as a tortilla to chew on. After the initial break, the mother does not offer her breast to the child again. The child will continue to sleep with the parents for a short time, but after weaning, he will sleep by the father rather than by the mother in order that he not be drawn to the mother's breast at night when he is in a sleepy state.

Excerpts from one of our interviews on weaning might provide some additional appreciation and insight into the attitudes of the mothers concerning weaning.

Q. How old was Abel when he was able to eat alone, that is, without aid?
A. He began to eat alone when he was nine months. I gave him his broth in a plate and he ate it. He picked up the plate and he also took his cup of water all by himself.
Q. How old was Abel when you ceased giving him the breast? Or, when he ceased nursing?
A. He was one and a half years old. As I have no children after him, he was the last.
Q. But before that you gave him a little bit to eat of other things?
A. Yes, I told you, he began to eat at four months of age.
Q. Did you take the breast from Abel little by little or in one fell swoop?
A. At one time.
Q. Did Abel not complain as you took the breast from him? Did he cry or yell?
A. Jesus, he didn't pay any attention. I put him to sleep with his eldest brother. He didn't even cry. Yes, he cried when he nursed because then he wanted something better to eat.
Q. Did you or did you not give him the breast again?
A. No more. I took it away all at one time and he didn't complain about it.
Q. Did you put anything or apply anything on the breast in order that Abel would not ask for it?
A. No. I tied up my breast so that he would not pay any attention. I tied it with a little handkerchief so that he wouldn't find my breast. Some people put saliva, that bitter herb on the breast, or they paint it with something,

that is, with some charcoal, but my son wasn't foolish and I didn't have to do that. He drank his atoli and ate his tortilla. I am too poor to give him cow's milk. Just hot tortilla and toli.

Q. Did you not give him something distasteful to eat when he asked for the breast in order that he would not ask for it again?

A. No, I didn't give it to him. I gave him sugar cane because that is good when one is taking the breast away from the child because it is sweet and has water. The child can chew it and they forget to want to nurse. When they cry one could clean off a piece of sugar cane and that should suffice. Then they forget they want to nurse.

Not all children take weaning so easily as Abel. Many mothers reported that the period following weaning was a difficult one. They reported that children cry more frequently during the two to six months following weaning, and the child experiences, for the first time, the discomfort of being allowed to cry on occasion without receiving as much nurturance as he would formerly have received. Before weaning, the infant would almost invariably be offered the breast or some other comfort when he was fussy or crying. During the transition period immediately after weaning, fussing or crying does not inevitably lead to being nurtured. An observation taken during a fiesta in which about 20 women were in the community house preparing food will illustrate this point. A small boy aged 3 was sitting by his mother, who had a 3-month-old infant strapped to her back in a rebozo. The boy had been weaned about six months earlier. The observation follows:

Juan is sitting by his mother's knee while she is sorting and cleaning beans. The mother gets up to go outside the room to change the infant's diaper (they do not change diapers in the room where there is food cooking). Juan begins to cry as the mother disappears out the door. He continues to cry and the mother does not return and he is crying loud enough for her to hear him outside. None of the other adults in the room offer him any assistance. He continues crying for four minutes and finally one of the other women tells him to keep quiet, that the mother will be back. Gradually he slows down and stops crying but continues to gulp sobs, and tears continue to run down his face. The mother becomes engaged in other activities outside the door and returns only after fifteen minutes. By this time Juan has stopped crying but still sobs intermittently. The mother goes over to him and he cuddles up against her. There are no words exchanged between them. The mother offers him a tortilla and sits quietly beside him and he leans against her and goes to sleep five minutes later. (When the mother returned, the infant was asleep in the rebozo on her back.)

This observation is not presented as representing the most typical behavior, since an examination of all of our observations taken on children in early childhood indicate that it is relatively rare for nurturance to be withheld for as long a period as indicated in the above account. The observation does illustrate, however, the insecurity of the child following weaning and also demonstrates the fact that several adults would withhold nurturance on occasion during that period. In a more typical situation in the household, the mother would withhold the nurturance formerly given, but she would encourage and insist on the older siblings providing the nurturance for the young child. They would see it as the duty of the older sisters and cousins to provide the care and nurturance of the young children. It is the mother's duty to care for the infant, but a mother cannot accomplish all her work if she has young children under foot also. In a real sense the mother is weaning the child away from herself as the major source of nurturance during the several months following actual weaning. For example, the mother no longer carries the child in the rebozo. Thus weaning involves physical separation as well as withdrawal of the breast. The transference of the primary caretaking responsibilities from the mother to the sibling group, however, is not an abrupt one like weaning from the breast. It takes place gradually, beginning at about the time the child is weaned. However, the child still continues to spend a good share of the time with his mother, and generally it is not until about a year after weaning that he spends almost all of his daytime hours with the older sibling caretakers.

In general, however, after weaning, the response to succorant appeals on the part of the child are less immediate, particularly if there is no apparent need. One very frequently reported undesirable behavior during early childhood is "crying without any reason." Several mothers reported that a young child who cries for some reason is immediately nurtured and comforted, and various attempts are made to alleviate his discomfort. But they also reported that when children cry without any reason, that is undesirable behavior. With the exception of two mothers of young girls, all the mothers of young children reported that they would either scold or physically punish such behavior. This report on the part of the mothers of the younger children corresponds with the observational material. The mothers believe that the frequency of crying without reason increases following weaning. The observational evidence indicates that this is a realistic appraisal by the mothers, although it does suggest that withholding of previously given nurturance, rather than punishment, is the most frequent response. Oddly enough, the mothers of older boys report that they would comfort the child, while the mothers of older girls report scolding or hitting as the main response. We do not have any adequate explanation for the responses of the mothers of the older boys.

Weaning is also related to the problem of health. The mothers report that this is a dangerous time from the point view of the health of the child. Given the rather poor diets of the barrio people, it is our impression that this period is indeed a dangerous time. The child's resistance to various kinds of ailments seems to be low in the months following weaning, and although we do not have definite figures to document this, it is our distinct impression that the frequency of illness during the year following weaning is relatively high compared to the year preceding and the years succeeding this period.

As nearly as we can tell from an examination of the observation protocols, no special stress is placed on obedience during early childhood. It is not until around the time when the child enters late childhood that special stress is placed on obedience. Although, in the interviews, the mothers reported that obedience is desirable for children of this age, from observation we would judge that this is more of an ideal value on the part of the mothers than it is a principle put into practice in the training of the child. A quote from an observation on a 3-year-old girl will serve to document this point. Six children between the ages of 3 and 8 are playing around a large rock at the side of a house in one of the larger compounds. Three separate piles of cornstalks are scattered around the rock. At the time the observation begins, some of the children are sweeping with the cornstalks while others are walking on the cornstalks or sitting on them.

Cortina (the 3-year-old subject of the observation) has been walking around the rock and now begins to collect some plain sticks from among the stalks. She stands alone at one side of the pile, cleaning a stick from its dried outer husk. She is very intent on her work. She has about five sticks cleaned in her hand. She then wanders away from the piles of cornstalks, still holding the sticks in her hands, and enters one doorway of the closest room. She comes out immediately with a small chair in one hand and the sticks in the other hand. At the corner of the house, Odilia (a female cousin, age 6) reaches for the chair and tries to pull it away from Cortina. Cortina turns her back and pulls the chair. Odilia lets go of the chair, and Cortina carries the chair around to the side of the house and puts it on the ground. Juana (another female cousin, age 7) is sweeping the ground close by where Cortina places the chair. As Juana begins to sweep closer to Cortina, Cortina picks up the chair in her hands and holds it waiting for Juana to finish sweeping. Cortina then puts the chair back on the ground. She leaves her chair with the sticks on the seat and goes in the house and brings out another chair. Cortina's father and a male compainion enter the compound and pass Cortina as she comes out with the chair. The father asks her to bring the chair over to the other room for his compadre to sit on. Cortina continues walking around to the side of the house with the chair. (It was not evident whether she didn't mind her father or was just going to get another chair.) She walks up to the chairs and sits on one as her father comes around and takes the other chair. He does not say anything, and neither does she. (There is no noise or crying or any special recognition as he takes the chair.)

The father's request for a chair, which was ignored in this case, seems like an ideal opportunity for obedience training if there were any stress on it at this age. This observation is quite typical, and we have several examples of parents making a request of a young child and not following up when the request was ignored. Almost never, during the earlier stages of early childhood, does either parent stress obedience in situations of this kind.

In the interviews, in contrast to the observations, mothers of girls reported that their children were obedient. In response to the question, "When you ask or tell your child to do something, does he do it right away, or does he delay?" five out of six of the mothers of young girls reported that their child obeyed right away. Mothers seemed to be more realistic about their sons' behavior, for four out of six of the mothers of the young boys indicated that their children would delay or not obey at all. The same contrast was noted in the answers of mothers of older children. In a mother's view, then, girls respond to requests or orders immediately, while boys delay or do not ever respond.

We also asked the mothers, "What do you do to your child if he delays?" Half the mothers of the younger boys responded that they would scold, and half responded that they would hit the child. This contrasts in an interesting way to the responses of the mothers with older boys, who unanimously reported scolding as the only technique of punishment. Mothers of girls reported equally as much scolding and hitting for both younger and older girls. The moderately frequent response of the mothers reporting the use of physical punishment did not correspond to the data gathered by observation. Not once during our entire stay did we see a parent strike a child. Since, in another context, every mother interviewed reported the use of physical punishment, there seems little doubt that on occasion parents do strike their children, but this is a relatively rare occurrence and probabaly takes place mostly in private.

In response to a general question on the technique of punishment preferred by the mothers of the younger children, we found that all but two said that scolding was a more frequent and preferred kind of punishment than physical punishment. Isolation of a young child was mentioned by four mothers as a form of punishment. It is conceived of as being relatively harsh and may be used on occasion if a child fights back. The report that physical punishment is more frequently used on younger boys than on older boys reflects the increasing differentiation in the treatment of boys and girls in late childhood. During early childhood it is apparent that boys and girls are treated very much the same, while, in the later stage, use of physical punishment is reported to continue for the girls but not for the boys. Our interpretation of the interview material, in conjunction with the observational data, is that obedience is ideally desirable from children in early childhood but that, in practice, it is seldom required or enforced. The mothers also stated that they used an embrace, praise, or material rewards for obedient behavior. The reported use of these various rewards for obedience was also greater than that which we noted in the observational protocols.

Returning to the observation reported above, the dominance-submission relationship between Odilia and Cortina should be noted. It will be remembered that Odilia, aged 6, reached for the chair Cortina, aged 3, carried and tried to pull it away. Cortina resisted and Odilia gave up. Obviously Odilia would have been physically able to take the chair away from Cortina. Situations of this sort almost never lead to any overt aggression or scuffle among children in this age group. Observations of many situations similar to this one indicate one of two outcomes. The first is the one observed in the above episode where Odilia reaches out for the chair and, when it is not proferred immediately, gives up the attempt to take it. The other outcome that we have frequently observed would be for Cortina to give Odilia the chair with no further comment. One could argue that the gesture of Odilia's putting her hand on the chair is a nonverbal request for the chair, in which case the nonverbal answer would be either "No" as in this case, or "Yes" if the request had been complied with. The important point is that these situations almost never lead to any further aggression. It should further be noted that the sex of the interactors does not seem to make any difference in the responses. In other words, had Odilia been a boy, Cortina's response would probably not have been any different; or contrariwise, had the younger child been a boy, one would not predict a different outcome.

A final aspect of the same observation that deserves attention is the nature of the activity of a group of young children. The activities are not organized or integrated in any way. The children are playing close to one another, but they do not have common goals, and the amount of social interaction is relatively small and diffuse. Organized games do not begin until late childhood. Further insight into obedience and types of playing may be gained from an observation taken of two children at the very end of the period of early childhood. The two girls are Elidia (age 6) and Juana (age 7). They are cousins living in the same household and are playing in the yard at what might be called making dinner or preparing food. They are playing under a tree close by a great-aunt (age 80) who is sitting under the tree, sewing. As the observation begins, Juana is trying to knock some dry leaves off the tree to crumble for the play food.

As Juana hits the branches of the tree with a stick, the dried leaves fall on the aunt and her work. The aunt tells Juana to stop hitting down the leaves, but Juana continues to knock down the leaves. Then the aunt asks Elidia to pick up the leaves that have fallen on the sewing materials of the aunt. Elidia comes around and picks them up off from the aunt's materials. Elidia then shows Juana what a big handful of leaves she has. Juana pays no apparent attention, continuing to hit the leaves down. Elidia takes some leaves in her skirt and goes over to the side wall of the house and makes a pile of them. Then she returns to the tree and points up to a big one telling Juana to get that one. Juana does not pay any attention. Elidia gets more leaves in her skirt and takes them back to her pile. Juana calls that there are some more to pick up on the other side of a big pile of logs. Elidia comes immediately and climbs over the pile of logs (with some difficulty) and picks up some more leaves. She walks back around the pile of logs carrying what she can. Juana calls that there are more, so Elidia returns close to Juana. At this point Juana walks away toward the house. Elidia tries to pick up all the leaves, but there are too many, and the wind keeps blowing them out of her hands. (She shows no visible reaction to the wind blowing the leaves.) She then gets an armload of leaves (rather than carrying them in her skirt as previously) and walks back with them around the logs to her original pile of leaves. She returns to pick up all the leaves that the wind hasn't blown away. She then forms a large neat pile of leaves and drops them through her hands. Juana returns with some pieces of old pottery to play with. Elidia offers Juana some leaves. (She points to the pile and says "Have some.") Juana takes about half the pile of leaves.

It is to be noted that the aunt places no special stress on insisting on obedience from Juana. Nor does she give any visible rewards to Elidia for compliance to her request to remove the leaves from her sewing materials. This lack of special attention to obedience during early childhood is quite representative of our other observation protocols. Again and again we have observed opportunities where obedience might appropriately be stressed in early childhood, but the occasions are not used to instill obedience in any way.

The amount of interaction between the children playing is also quite typical in this observation. Relatively little conversation goes on between children of this age, and although they are playing in a common area and with similar materials, the amount of interaction in any organized way is small. The slightly older girl, Juana, does initiate more suggestions than does Elidia. In terms of caretaking duties, Juana is just entering the stage of late childhood. Since there are other older girls in the same household, however, Juana is not really being pressed into a caretaking role in any important way at the time of the observation.

Children in early childhood spend most of their time playing in the courtyard with siblings and cousins. In light of this fact, the responses reported below of mothers to the interview question as to whether they preferred their children to play alone or with others were surprising. Fifty percent of the mothers reported that they would prefer their children to play alone. Both sex and age of child made a difference in the response received from the mother. The older the child, the more frequent would be the response of preferring the child to play alone, and this response was also more frequent from mothers of girls than it was from mothers of boys. One third of the mothers of young boys and one half of the mothers of young girls preferred them to play alone. This difference between boys and girls is even more striking in the older age group of late childhood. There, one third of the mothers of boys reported they would prefer them to play alone, while all but one of the mothers of girls so reported. The reasons given by the mothers for this preference indicated that it was mainly desirable because it cut down on the probability of ordering other children around or of getting into a fight. Since all of the mothers are very concerned and preoccupied about any aggressive behavior, we interpret their responses as indicating a high value on avoiding any situation involving the possibility of such behavior. Thus the ideal statement shows a preference for playing alone despite the fact that in reality the children are almost always playing with close relatives. This anxiety concerning aggression undoubtedly does affect the amount of play allowed by the mothers with other than very close relatives. Our observational material clearly demonstrates that play groups for both early and late childhood are composed almost exclusively of children who are closely related and very seldom include distant relatives or any other outsiders.

The mothers' concern about aggression is further revealed by an analysis of the responses to the following question, "What do you wish your child to do if another child looks for an argument with him and when the other child wishes to fight with him?" All of the mothers of young children indicated that they would want their child to come home immediately if anyone attempted to pick a fight with him. Almost all of the mothers of early-childhood children indicated that they would use hitting as punishment to prevent their child from fighting back when attacked. There was only one mother in the entire sample who would encourage her child to fight back, and she was the mother of one of the older boys. She was also the only mother in our sample who had not been born in the barrio. Her responses to several questions concerning aggression and achievement were different from those of any of the other mothers. To prevent fighting back was the only reason for which almost all of the mothers reported that they would use physical punishment. This again points up the special concern with aggressive behavior. We also asked the mothers what sort of punishment they would use if a child attempted to order around other children of his own age. Such behavior was thought to be undesirable by all of the mothers, and all but one reported that they would use scolding as the technique of punishment. The sex of the child would make no difference in the treatment for either fighting back or ordering others around. This is further evidence for the relative lack of differentiation between the training of the two sexes during early childhood. As we shall see in the next chapter, the differentiation between sexes begins to assume importance only at the beginning of late childhood.

The major part of "early childhood," then, is spent in the courtyard. Occasionally the child may accompany an older caretaker to the outskirts of the barrio, where the older siblings and cousins may be engaged in washing clothes or taking baths. The confinement to the courtyard cannot be explained by realistic fears on the part of parents, for the environment in the barrio is on the whole a benign one. There are no poisonous snakes or insects in the area, nor are there any dangerous wild animals. The oxen which are frequently herded through the streets of the barrio are very difficult to turn. Children are taught to keep out of their way and must get into a doorway or step inside a gate. All adults and older children will, if necessary, move to help them out of the way.

Only during parts of the rainy season is the child very frequently in physical discomfort. Then he may be drenched in sudden rainstorms if he is not in the courtyard. When he gets wet, he seldom has other clothes to change into and may become chilled and cold.

About a year after weaning, there are a series of new skills to be learned by the young child. These include such things as learning to dress and to urinate and defecate by themselves. The big majority of the mothers of young children reported that their children learned to urinate and defecate by themselves around age 3. (The mothers of the older children reported that their children learned this at age 2. We would interpret this reported difference as a drift in the mothers' memories rather than an indication of a real change in the age of training.) Since there is a complete lack of sanitation facilities in the village, toilet training is a relatively casual affair and is not given any special attention. Toilet training consists of learning to go to a particular part of the patio and to perform one's duties there rather than elsewhere in the patio. When not at home, it requires only that one step into a relatively unobtrusive place in order to perform one's duties. One is not supposed to defecate in the street but, rather, to step into the fields or at least off the path. Indians who come into town from the surrounding mountain areas are thought to be rather uncouth because they do defecate in the streets.

Toilet training begins after the child learns to walk and the mother takes him outside the house. "They learn to walk, then one teaches them, and they go out alone." All but three of the children in the sample were trained by 3 years of age. Urination just outside the doorway comes first, and then gradually the child learns to go out to the fields or to a corner of the patio alone for either function. Young children are usually without pants at this age, and training is rather simple. Most mothers said that they would talk to the child or scold him for errors, but others said that they did nothing, for the child would gradually learn anyhow.

The ability to dress oneself is acquired shortly after the toilet training takes place, generally between the third and fourth year of life. There are no reported differences in the age at which boys and girls acquire this skill. Since they sleep fully clothed, there is not any early morning rush to clothe oneself. On arising, a little girl shakes out her rebozo and wraps it around her shoulders and head. A small boy shakes out his hat, places it on his head, and is ready to start the day. If a change of clothing is necessary and available during the day, children are generally able to change without help by the age of 4.

In the interviews, the mothers of the younger children reported that these youngsters, both boys and girls, have few assigned duties and are treated with relatively great leniency. "They should play when they want to and help when they want to." The early tasks for young girls include going to get water with the mother or older sibling, piling up dishes after meals, learning about fire care by bringing wood and blowing on the fire, and running small errands. Before girls are strong enough to carry heavy water buckets or do grinding, they learn the correct posture and methods through imitative play. There is no caretaking in this group except perhaps to be nurturant to even younger siblings, but these girls do not have any responsibility for babies as yet. Boys in early childhood are starting to learn animal care and feeding and may walk with the father to nearby fields. They also run errands for the mother.

Most of their simple tasks are more in the nature of imitative behavior of the older siblings and cousins. Helping by young children often takes the form of apparently spontaneous help without being asked or without any kind of formal or overt instruction. An example of this is given in an excerpt from one of the observations on Antonia, age 5. Antonia's older half-sister, age 13, is sweeping the room when the observation begins, and Antonia is standing just outside the door.

As Aulalia finishes sweeping out the room, she begins piling dirt onto a mat and then folding the sides of the mat up together. Antonia runs, without anyone's saying anything to her, and lifts up the mat. She rolls it up and puts it on her head with the waste inside and walks over to the corner of the patio and dumps the dirt out of the mat and shakes the mat. She returns with the mat on her head and then throws it onto the floor in the middle of the room. She bends over, and with her hand brings together a small bit of trash that remains in the corner. Her younger sister, aged $1\frac{1}{2}$, comes and attempts to help her. Antonia pushes her sister's hand away, gathers the trash into her own hand, and walking toward the door, she throws it outside. The wind carries the trash away.

The differential assignment of tasks according to sex of child is not drawn during early childhood. Boys of this age frequently do little tasks that are later assigned to girls as serious work. For example, carrying water is considered mainly a girl's task, as is sweeping. But little boys will participate in imitative activities of these sorts at an early age, when later he will not engage in such female tasks. In summary, the observational material quite definitely indicates that early childhood is pretty much free from any responsibilities for regular and serious tasks. It is sufficient that a young child not be a burden to his mother in terms of requiring time and attention and that he learn to play and to accept the caretaking of older female relatives. Our individual ratings show no difference in the responsible behavior of girls and boys at this age. There is some indication, however, that girls are already being trained for their future caretaking roles.

On the basis of our ratings, nurturance is the only behavior system in which we can detect a difference between boys and girls in early childhood. On the average, girls show many more nurturant responses than do boys of this age. There is also a relationship between the amount of nurturance shown and the age of the child. In general, there is a gradual increase in the amount of nurturance through the period of early childhood. Girls tend to show the nurturant responses earlier than do the boys. By the time late childhood begins, both boys and girls show a high frequency of nurturant responses. Thus during early childhood the difference between the boys' behavior and the girls' behavior is accounted for by the fact that the girls begin to show more nurturant behavior at an earlier age than do the boys. When it is considered that the girls will take on caretaking responsibilities at an early age, it is reasonable that their training with respect to the behavior system of nurturance would begin earlier than that for the boys.

Socialization of various kinds of sex behavior, including such things as modesty and imitative sex play and masturbation, is handled in a rather casual way during early childhood. There are no specific or severe rules concerning any of these activities at the beginning of early childhood. A young child may go around nude without causing any special comment or evoking any punishment or discipline from the caretaker. In contrast, during the latter part of early childhood, children will be lightly ridiculed for going around nude. Thus there is a gradual learning process regarding modesty during early childhood.

Masturbation and imitative sex play between small children are treated with equal casualness. Parents and caretakers tend to be very permissive concerning these activities at the beginning of early childhood and gradually extinguish such activities, mainly through ridicule, toward the end of that stage. The observations of these activities indicate that masturbation and imitative sex play are not particularly common although by no means unusual. The following observation provides insight into the attitudes concerning imitative sex play. This is an observation of 6-year-old Marina, who is playing in the patio with her 4-year-old brother, Alfonso, and her younger sister Chlorea, who is about 2. The three children are playing in sight of their mother and an aunt, who are sitting just inside the doorway sewing.

Marina draws close to Chlorea and says, "Now I will carry you." She stands Chlorea up, bends over, and takes Chlorea by the arms and carries her on her back and runs over to Alfonso. When Marina arrives in the middle of the patio, she throws herself to the ground and the two little girls fall into a sitting position. Marina laughs, saying, "Aye, yi, yi," as if she were very tired. (*Note:* She does this in jest, as in a game.) She gets up and takes Chlorea by the hand and steps toward the door. She then again picks up Chlorea and walks around the patio with her. She again throws both of them on the ground laughing. The two of them lay on their backs and both laugh, breathing hard from the play. Alfonso comes toward her and takes off his cotton trousers that he had on. He stands there nude and then throws the trousers over Marina. Marina gets up on her hands and feet, covered with the trousers and she cries, "Oh," from underneath them. Then she uncovers herself, sits down, and then stands up laughing. Alfonso throws himself upon her and cries, "Now I've got you," and the two children roll around on the ground kicking and laughing. Chlorea has gone a few steps away. Chlorea picks up a rock from the patio and puts it into her mouth. Marina watches, stands up and walks over to Chlorea, taking the stone away from her and hitting her on the hand, saying to her very seriously, "You shouldn't eat that." Chlorea begins to cry. Marina runs and again throws herself on Alfonso, and they whirl around on the ground. A teenage girl standing at the edge of the patio says, "Hurry up, Chlorea, run and hit Marina." At that moment Arelia Grusmon (mother of Marina) comes into the patio. She is carrying a basket. Marina stands up laughing, jumps on one foot, and cries, "Ah, my mother's come." Arelia goes into the cook shack. Marina returns and throws herself on Alfonso, who is lying on the ground still naked. The two children roll around laughing. Marina puts her finger in Alfonso's anus and laughing hits him with the other hand. The boy pulls her hair. She squeezes the boy's testicles with her hand and cries, "I'm going to hit you on the rear end." She laughs. Alfonso sits up and, also laughing, hits Chlorea lightly on the head. (Chlorea had stopped crying and had approached the other two children.) The little girl starts to cry again. Marina puts her arms about her and caresses her head; then Marina looks at Alfonso as if she were angry and says, "Go on, you donkey, get up." Alfonso again throws himself on her, and the two roll around on the ground laughing.

Two or three items of interest occur in this observation. In the first place, the amount of activity and physical exertion engaged in by the children is greater than is typical on the basis of other observations. This activity and excitement also affect the children's behavior toward their 2-year-old younger sister. Typically they would not allow the younger sister to cry, nor would they aggress against her even in jest. Marina's instruction to her younger sister about eating a rock is typical behavior and could be documented in many other observations. However, one would have expected her to nurture the baby after instructing her concerning the stone. The activity of the two children is undoubtedly related to the kind of sex play in which they were engaged and led to a somewhat higher amount of activity and excitement than is typical. This was generally true of the few cases we observed of imitative sex behavior. It should also be noted that there were older people, including adults, around who had seen Alfonso naked and who saw Marina and Alfonso playing together on the ground. None of these people took any steps to interfere or to interrupt the activity. Judging from other observations, it would be our guess that in about two years they will begin to ridicule behavior of this kind.

In summary, early childhood involves weaning, toilet training, learning to dress and feed oneself, learning to play with other children, and not to make too many demands on parents and adults. There is little perceived difference in the treatment of boys and girls, and the only area where sex difference in behavior was obvious was in the higher frequency of nurturant responses in girls.

In rating the children on the behavior systems, there were one or two findings with respect to the ratings that merit interest. The first of these was the discovery that frequently children from related households tended to cluster together on the ratings to a rather marked degree. This strongly suggests that if we had fine enough measuring instruments, we would be able to detect family differences in child-training practices. It is true that there may be some con-tamination effect of our ratings of closely related people; however, it is our strong belief that there are definite clusterings of child-training practices by various large extended families in the barrio. We were able to trace the genealogical connections among all of the 22 intensively studied families. We were then able to rate the degree of relationship between various clusters of families. An analysis of the ratings indicates that family differences account for a great deal of the variability of our ratings. In those behavior systems where there was no significant difference by sex or age of the child, the family differences accounted for most of the observed variability.

At one point in our analysis we attempted to distinguish between those children who were reared in nuclear families and those who were reared in extended families. It was our impression at the time that some of the children were reared in nuclear families. A closer analysis of the residence patterns and the interaction patterns between related families revealed, however, that none of the children in our sample were reared in a nuclear family situation. Even in cases where only one family lived in a compound, it turned out, on closer scrutiny, that closely related families lived very close by and that in fact the children of early childhood age were part of a group formed by the siblings and cousins and other close relatives. The social context for the children was equivalent to an extended family in all cases when judged on the criterion of interaction during the day and with caretakers.

We also attempted an analysis of the possible effects of position in birth order on the various ratings of the behavior systems. Because of the fluid residence patterns and the amount of interaction with other families who were closely related, we were unable to make any very clear-cut conclusions about the effect of birth order. The one exception to this pertains to the terminal child in a family. The last child in a family tends to enter the various stages at a somewhat older age than is true for other children. An example of this is the age of weaning, as reported earlier. The last child tends to be weaned later. The last child also tends to be trained later with respect to self-reliance, succorance, obedience, nurturance, and responsibility. No effects were detectable for dominance.

♉
♉
♉

Chapter 13

Late Childhood

Although the transition from early to late childhood is difficult to pinpoint precisely in time, its implications for the child are dramatic in several respects. At the age of 5 or 6, the child encounters changes in the daily round of activities and increasing demands for participation in the simpler household tasks and the care of younger siblings. There are new patterns of interaction to be learned in school and with the Mexican children in the central part of town. Even more important are the adjustments to changing parental expectations that are supported by the withdrawal of earlier nurturance, changes in techniques of discipline, and increasing demands for responsibility and obedience. Clear cut differences in the socialization of males and females also appear with explicit clarity at this period of life.

It must be emphasized that the transition is not abrupt. Unlike the almost overnight transition from infancy to early childhood, the change from early to late childhood is gradual and generally takes two to three years to complete. It typically begins during the fifth year, although it varies from one child to another. In general, parents begin training girls earlier than boys. Similarly, they tend to postpone these demands and expectations for youngest children. Later in the chapter it will be seen that these variations are related to the need for labor to perform various household tasks, and that the age of transition depends, in part, on the family's labor requirements.

The parents' conception of the nature of the child at this stage differs in some important respects from the concept of the child in early childhood. Probably the most important is the idea that the child now has *reason*. Whereas earlier he could learn only by imitation, now he can be taught by reason and counsel as well and can understand the place his tasks have in the family and in life generally. A second idea is that the child at this stage is most malleable and teachable. Later he will become set and independent in his ways. Although youths are still somewhat teachable, it is felt that now is the ideal time to instill proper work habits.

The child's conception of himself reflects his new status. While the transition from early childhood is rather difficult with respect to the behavior systems of nurturance and succorance, the transition into appropriate and responsible role behavior seems to be rather smooth. When tasks are assigned to children of this age, they are generally discharged without any particular fuss or bother, although not always with any great speed. There are many behavioral indications that the child wants to join older people in their tasks and identifies with the roles of people older than themselves.

Probably the most pervasive and overt change is the nature of the participation in the daily round of activities; the part played and the tasks required in late childhood differ from those of early childhood in several important respects. Unlike the rather passive accepting position of the earlier period, these children, particularly the girls, become active participants with a variety of assigned tasks. Since these tasks occur throughout the day and are not limited to any particular time or activity, we shall describe them and the techniques used by parents to assure their performance.

In contrast to early childhood when the list of tasks was small, relatively undifferentiated with respect to sex, and seen by parents as practice for later responsibility, the tasks of late childhood are many, differentiated with respect to sex, and seen by parents as real contributions to the family labor supply. The girls' tasks mentioned most, in the mother interviews, in order of frequency and importance in terms of time, included the following: caring for younger siblings, carrying water, running errands that involve food, or going to market, keeping the fire, caring for small domestic animals such as turkeys and chickens, sweeping and other household tasks, serving food and washing small dishes, bathing self and younger siblings, and washing small items. Cooking, care of large cooking pots, heavy washing, and grinding of corn are not required until later. Boys' tasks include, in rough order of importance, gathering produce or fodder in the fields and bringing it to the house, care of large animals such as goats and burros, some light work in the fields, gathering firewood in close by hills and keeping wood neat in the courtyard, and running errands of various sorts. In general, the girls' tasks at this stage are greater in number and more time consuming. In families where there are no girls, the boys are usually expected to do some tasks normally reserved for girls, especially caretaking of younger siblings, caring for small domestic animals, and sweeping. The reverse is not usually true; if there are no boys in the family, the boys' tasks are done by the male head of the household or a male relative.

The kinds of tasks performed by older children and the differences between early and late childhood can best be illustrated from the observations. The following sequence was observed in the kitchen of the Ramos house, where Helena, age 8, is behind her mother, who is grinding corn for tortillas. Helena is sitting, leaning against the wall with her feet stretched out in front of her, eating a tortilla.

Helena's mother asks her to take a cup of water to her father. The child gets up, takes a cup from a box, comes up to the earthen pot, and crouching down, fills the cup from the water in the pot.

With the tortilla in one hand and the cup of water in the other, she goes out into the couryard. Since the door is closed, in order to open it she kicks it with her foot. The door bolts open. The child, back facing the kitchen, pulls the door again with her foot, and kicks it back to close it.

Helena walks toward the entrace of the room where her father, with another man, is making a drain ditch so that the rain water will not run into the room. The other man is her uncle.

In silence, she hands her father the cup with the water. Her father takes it, looking at the child without saying anything to her, and he drinks. The child stands there with her hands hanging down watching him drink as if she were waiting for something. Her father stops drinking and puts the cup on the ground while he talks with her uncle about the drain. Helena crouches down, picks up the cup from the ground, throws the remaining water on the ground, and runs back to the kitchen with the cup in hand.

She enters the kitchen, opening the door and leaving it open. She returns to the place she was before. She leaves the cup on the ground next to her and sits down behind her mother. She eats her tortilla in silence. Into the kitchen comes Helena's younger brother, who asks for a chair. Helena's mother looks at her and repeats the request. Helena gets up slowly. She takes a few steps and takes a small chair in one hand (in the other, she still has the tortilla) and carries it on her back as far as the child. She sets the chair down and remains standing looking at it. Her younger brother sits in the little chair, smiling.

Helena, with the same serious expression on her face, returns to where she was before, sits down, and continues to eat the tortilla.

The following observation illustrates the girl's part in helping with food preparation. It takes place in the cook shack of the Gutierrez family. Just outside the door, Mr. Gutierrez is talking to a neighbor woman who has come to buy corn. Juanita, age 7, is sitting in a corner behind the fire, cleaning beans by passing them from hand to hand and blowing across them. Across the room from her and close to the fire sit the mother, Manuela Gutierrez, and two younger sisters of Juanita, ages 2 and 4, who are sitting passively.

Juanita passes the beans from hand to hand three times. When she has finished this, she stretches and shakes her skirt, which has some dirt on it. She then takes a peach from the ground next to her, cleans it with her hand, and bites into it. She puts the peach down on top of the clean beans in the pot. She squats down on the ground and, with one hand, retrieves the beans which have fallen on the mat on which she has been sitting. She throws these beans with the rest into the pot and takes the peach, sighs, bites it, and stands up. With her left hand (in her right hand she has the peach), she cleans her skirt by shaking it.

She crosses the room, going toward a large basket, and fills her skirt with beans. She returns to the place where she was before, sits down, puts the peach on top of the pot of clean beans, smooths her hair down with her hands, makes her feet comfortable, picks up the peach and takes another bite.

For the first time Juanita looks at the group which is formed by her mother and her little sisters. The youngest sister had just asked for the mother's breast and the mother did not wish to give it to her, and the group had been laughing about this. Juanita shakes her hair with one hand, grabs a fist full of beans and begins cleaning them again. The mother stands up and, crossing in front of her, looks at her. In order to pass, the mother picks up the pot of beans and puts it on top of the metate and then is standing between the metate and Juanita with her back to the little girl. Juanita says in a gentle voice, "The pot." The mother, without turning around, asks, "What, my little daughter?" and Juanita repeats her request for the pot. The mother, without looking at her, hands her the pot of beans with one hand behind her, still with her back to the little girl. Juanita takes the pot, puts it to one side, opposite to where it had been before. She continues cleaning the beans.

The mother crosses to the other side of the room and sits down. Juanita remains crouched and reaches her arm over to hand the pot of clean beans to her mother without speaking. After Juanita hands the pot of beans to her mother, she stands up, scratches her arm, and goes to a corner, picking up a jar of water and handing it to her mother. The mother receives it and begins to clean the beans with water. Juanita remains looking at her. The mother says to her, "Hand me the dirty plates." Juanita takes two steps toward the metate and picks up a pile of dirty plates, which she hands to her mother. The mother takes the plates and says, "Bring me water." Juanita walks toward the pail. The mother says, "Not that pail over there. Over here." Juanita goes to the other pail, fills a gourd full of water (the gourd was floating in the pail of water), and takes it over to her mother, putting it on the ground next to the dirty plates.

There are several typical features to note about these two observations. First, there are constant demands made on the girls by their parents, especially by the mother. These requests are constant in contrast to the period of early childhood when few demands were made. Second, the parents make few nurturant responses toward the children in late childhood in contrast to their constant nurturant responses in the earlier periods. In the first observation above, it is interesting that Helena was required to comply with, or nurture, the requests of her younger brother by giving him a chair. Here the young child is gratified by the expenditure of the older child's effort. A third feature to note in both observations is that little reward is offered for the proper execution of tasks. Helena's father ignored her, and any expectation she may have had of appreciation for her behavior was disappointed. Similarly, Juanita received no overt special thanks for her work.

Before turning to the question of how such compliant behavior is learned, an illustration of typical tasks performed by boys of this age will be useful. The following episode involves three older boys, ages 7 to 9, engaged in the task of carrying corn husks from town to the barrio for feed for cattle.

Franco is sitting on the edge of the sidewalk with his cousin, Angel Chavez, waiting for his other cousin, Margerito Chavez, who is in a small store buying something. Next to the children is a great bundle of corn husks which they are watching while Margarito returns with the donkey.

Margarito arrives with the donkey and stands at the corner in front of the door where the corn husks are piled. He looks at the children and says, "Let's go." Then he looks at Angel and says, "Toss it to me," and points to the husks. Angel stands up and lifts the pile of husks, carrying it with difficulty. Franco, with a stick in his mouth, watches the proceedings.

When the children have placed the husks on top of the donkey, Franco stands up and comes close, rubbing the head of the animal and embracing his snout while pulling on the lead rope. The donkey moves, and the husks appear to be about ready to fall off. Margarito grabs them quickly and says, "Hey, grab the rope, Franco." Franco fastens the rope, rolling it up in his hand while the other children finish tying the husks on top of the donkey.

Franco leans over the head of the animal and asks, "All ready?" "All ready," answers Margarito, "Let's go." Margarito turns the donkey around, pulling it into the middle of the street, gives a little jump, and climbs on to the rear end of the animal. Franco runs behind and fastens a strap that passes over the tail of the animal, tightening the saddle.

Margarito gets the animal moving while Franco is running behind and finishing the tightening of the ropes. Then the donkey stops. Franco comes close and puts one hand on the saddle while the other is hanging onto Margarito's pants. He sticks one foot in the stirrup and gives a jerk with his body that pulls him up and climbs onto the donkey, sitting behind Margarito. With one hand he strikes the animal, who starts running through the streets toward the barrio, while Angel, on foot, runs behind.

These new duties are associated with various new techniques of discipline. In general, there is a great increase in the ratio of punishments to rewards. Whereas in early childhood, rewards and nurturance for compliance were the major techniques for training, in late childhood, punishment for lack of compliance becomes more prevalent. The child is now considered capable of understanding and is therefore punished for failure to carry out requests or commands, as well as being subjected to withdrawal of nurturant responses by the parent. Consider the following observation, for example.

Helena, age 8, is sitting on a small chair while her Aunt Rosa, age 9, stands behind her picking lice out of her hair. Helena squirms around in the chair. Rosa jerks on her hair to make her sit still. As Rosa pulls her hair, Helena turns her head and looks at Rosa sideways. Rosa says to her, "Sit still."

Helena's mother comes out of the cook shack and shouts to Helena that the turkeys are out in the street. Helena looks at her but remains sitting in the chair and waits to be deloused. A minute or two passes, and then Helena's father comes out of the kitchen and approaches Helena, telling her in a rather serious tone that the turkeys have escaped. Helena gets up and runs out to the street. A half a block away are the turkeys. Helena runs up the street until she comes to them.

When she gets up to the turkeys, she waves her arms and shouts at them in order to scare them in the direction of the house. She runs back and forth from one side of the street to the other, herding the turkeys in front of her. One of the turkeys attempts to escape into some plants at the side of the road. Helena crouches down, picks up a stick, and with it in her hand, strikes the bird, forcing it to go with the others. With the stick in one hand and waving her arms, she has the turkeys jumping around in the mud in the street and coming back toward the house. She herds them into the courtyard and goes up to the door of the living room and says, "Shall I leave them?" "No," says her mother. Helena continues waving her arms and herds the birds into another corner of the courtyard. She then turns them around and herds them into the house. The turkeys enter the room, making a great deal of noise. Helena throws the stick away and leans into the cook shack, looks inside, and then crosses the courtyard and goes to stand in front of her father without speaking to him. She looks at him. Her father goes into the room without saying anything. Helena looks at the turkeys and then counts them to see if they are all there. She again approaches her father and looks at him. He does not speak or recognize her presence by any overt move.

This observation illustrates the use of a threat of punishment for noncompliance and the lack of a reward, nurturant or otherwise, by the adults for the completion of the task. In the interviews, there are many examples of the mothers' indicating that caresses, embraces, and other nurturant responses are not given as rewards to late-childhood children as frequently as they were given in early childhood. For example, one mother, when asked what she does when her child complies with a request, answered:

Now that she's older, we don't kiss her any more. We don't embrace her. Her father does occasionally when he feels like it. I don't do it any more as I have two other children. When her papa asks her for something and she brings it to him, he might say to her, "Daughter, I like that."

Answers such as this, on the part of several of the mothers in the interviews, indicate that there is an explicit awareness that cuddling, embracing, and other forms of physical nurturance are no longer appropriate for children in late childhood. It should be noted, however, that obedience and the mastery of these new skills are not expected until later. Obedience to the father is learned earlier than obedience to the mother; the child always complies with the father's commands more rapidly than with the mother's commands. This is associated with the fact that he is more consistent in backing up every request with punishment for noncompliance. The mothers, on the other hand, are less consistent in following up their commands and not infrequently allow noncompliance to go without any disciplinary action, or they delay punishment much longer than the father does. Fathers demand obedience equally from sons and daughters. Mothers, on the other hand, tend to let sons "get away" with more than daughters.

The two following observations both involve mother-child interactions. The first illustrates a request to a daughter and the second, a request to a son. Neither observation involves punishment but illustrates, rather, the degree of leeway allowed before any disciplinary actions are taken, and, equally important, the difference between the obedience expected from boys and girls—boys responding more slowly and with less apparent interest.

Juanita comes in from the street and stands in the doorway of the cook shack, looking silently at her mother. She stays this way for a little while. Then Juanita looks at her mother and says, "Mama, this Socorro (little sister) doesn't want to take a bath." Juanita's mother ceases grinding and looks at Juanita, saying, "Tell her to hurry up; tell her to bathe." Juanita answers, "But she says she is going to wash her head." Juanita's mother replies, "Tell her, not now, tell her to hurry up and come."

Juanita remains standing, looking at her mother without moving. Her mother begins to grind, and then she raises her head and says again, "Go on, go on and tell her to hurry up, that I'm about to leave." Juanita enters the cook shack, walking toward her mother; she stops half way between the door and where her mother is sitting and asks her mother, "Where are you going?" Her mother answers, "Go on, tell her to hurry up now, that I have to take the food out." Juanita smiles and says, "Where?" Her mother answers rapidly, "I'm going up to the woods." (That is, the mother is going up on the hillside.)

Juanita walks toward the door and stops and leans against the door frame with her arms at her back. Suddenly she says, "I'm going now." She begins to run toward the street. She stops in the middle of the patio and looks at the back of the cook shack, then goes on, walking slowly. She crosses the street in front of her house and goes along a little path; then she walks along through the corn field. She walks along looking at the ground. After about a hundred yards, she comes to a water ditch where her aunt, her mother's sister, is washing. And Socorro, Juanita's sister, is completely dressed in the water ditch, washing her head. Before reaching her, Juanita moves her arms and cries out, "Socorro, run; Mama says she is going to take the meal out to the hill." Socorro straightens up while the soapy water drips down and asks, "Who went out to plant?" Juanita says, "No one; I didn't say anything to Mother, but she said that you should hurry." Juanita's aunt looks at the girls and then goes back to her washing.

In the above observation, we see the mother repeating several times a request to a daughter to take a message to a younger sibling. It is typical that the mothers frequently speak to their daughters more than once before the daughters carry out a command. However, most such episodes result in the daughter carrying out the request of the mother. Contrast this observation with the one below describing an interaction between a mother and son. In it, the mother repeats a request several times, and the son avoids carrying out the request of the mother. In this episode, Jubenal, aged 8, and his mother, with the baby, are sitting on a log in the open courtyard. His mother is picking over ripe tomatoes from a basket. She has just returned from the field where she has picked them.

Jubenal is squatted beside his mother, eating a tomato. He is holding it in his hands and eating it very carefully, taking small bites, letting the juice drip between his legs on the ground. His mother does not say anything and continues to place the tomatoes into two piles, one of ripe tomatoes and the other of green. She gets several ripe ones ready for cooking in one spot. Jubenal reaches his hand over to take another tomato, and his mother says, "Go get me that pot." Jubenal says, "Where is it?" and continues eating. He is now eating the second tomato that he took. His mother says, "It's inside the cook shack." He turns around without getting up, and it does not seem to be in sight. (They are outside, not inside the cook shack.) He seems to search for it with his eyes, but can't find it. His mother gives him a prod with her elbow and says, "Go look."

He gets up, wiping his hands on the back of his pants, and walks very slowly over to the door of the cook shack. He pokes his head inside, leaning on the door jamb, and peers around in what must be a dark room after the bright sunlight. He comes back and squats down beside his mother, reaching his hand for another tomato, and says, "I can't find it." His mother continues separating the tomatoes and says, "Oh, pshaw, now go and look. I told you right where it was in the corner of the cook shack." Jubenal remains for a moment to finish the tomato and then wipes the juice with the back of his hands and stands up quickly and runs to the cook shack and enters and fumbles around inside. He sticks his head out the door and says, "Where is it?" His mother says, "Just look." He turns back into the room and seems to continue searching. He was turning over mats and looking under them and could not seem to find any pot. (Pots are never kept under mats, which lie flat on the ground.)

His mother remains outside, separating the tomatoes for the next five minutes. During this time Jubenal remains inside the cook shack but does not look for the pot any further. His mother, when she has finished sorting the tomatoes, goes back and walks in, lifts up a little basket and picks up the exact pot that she wants. She gives him a look in the eye that is almost a grin and then turns and walks back outside. Jubenal grins at her, but no words are spoken.

The above two observations illustrate two general differences between boys and girls in late childhood with respect to obedience in parent-child interaction. In many of the observations, we encountered the sequence where a mother requests something of a daughter and repeats the request, but each time the request is repeated, it tends to get stronger and stronger until the daughter complies. The pattern with a son is very different in that, in general, the son either complies after being asked a few times or else worms his way out entirely. Mothers, with their sons, are not so likely to increase the strength of the request, although this does occur on occasion. Another feature that recurs is the flaunting, by a son, of the mother's authority in a mild, but definitely interpretable manner, as shown in the above observation where the son pretends to look for the pot, but it is rather clear that the mother, as well as the son, realizes that he is not making a serious attempt to comply with the mother's request and, in fact, succeeds in not complying at all.

Two factors would seem to be related to this difference in the behavior between boys and girls. The first would be the reality factor that a girl's tasks are more closely related to the needs of the household, which the mother is running, that is, the kinds of tasks that a daughter does for her mother may in some ways be more necessary to running the household than are the expected and accepted tasks for boys. The second factor that accounts for the difference in behavior between boys and girls of this age is the expected deference shown to adults. Girls are expected to be more deferent to adults than are boys of this age. This is certainly, at least in part, preparation for the adult roles, but it also reflects the somewhat earlier and stricter obedience training for girls. The two observations below illustrate this difference very clearly, for the settings are similar and involve deference to adults shown by a girl (in the first example) and then by a boy (second example).

Antonia is standing by a partially opened door, listening to loud music coming from a phonograph. (*Note:* this is an old, hand-wind type with an amplifier, like the RCA dog ad, but it is something very new to this area.) Antonia sways back and forth to the music, not tapping her feet, but keeping time with over-all body movements. Antonia leans back against the doorway and gradually slides to a squatting position. She cocks her head on one side, seeming to listen to the music. An adult male friend of the family visiting the household goes to the half open door and starts to go out and then looks down at Antonia at his feet and says, "Move, child," but not harshly. Antonia quickly scoots over to one side, and he pushes the door completely open and steps outside. Antonia moves back into the better position to see the proceedings as he leaves, still squatting. Some people step up to the doorway (but don't come in, just look), and Antonia quickly moves back to the other side of the door. As they leave, she scoots back against the wall in the semidarkness of the room away from the open doorway. She sits down flat with her legs stretched out in front of her.

Compare the above example of deferent behavior on the part of a girl to a similar situation for Pedro. The following observation is taken during the day of the first harvest, which is a ceremonial and gay occasion. It takes place at the doorway of the cook shack in Pedro's household. There are many women around the house getting the food prepared to carry out to the field where the men have been working since early morning.

Pedro is sitting in the doorway where anyone entering or leaving the house must step over him. Many adult women, including his mother and aunt, are present. Pedro is leaning against the door jamb. This step is high, and his feet hang down inside the room. Pedro has one hand inside his pants. His head is on one side against the door. His eyes are half-closed, and he is making a choo-choo sound, something like a train.

Three women step over him, one at a time. Their long skirts brush against his legs. He doesn't move or appear to notice all the movement around him as his mother hands out baskets of food for the women to carry out into the field. He takes his hand out of his pants and wipes his nose with the back of it and then he turns over onto his stomach and hangs over the door sill, half inside and half outside, his feet hanging inside.

One woman stands at his head outside the room looking in, and her skirt almost covers his head. Three women go out the door, each lifting her skirt and stepping up over Pedro. One leans down and pats his head. He does not move or even look at her. He stays on the doorstep, and a dog from outside comes up and sniffs at him. He still doesn't move.

Pedro's sister comes up to the doorway and says to the mother, "I'm going to the field now," and turns back to the patio. Pedro gets up slowly, looks after her as she crosses the yard, and then runs after her saying, "Me, me." The sister walks to the side of the wall and gets a basket which she intends to fill with food. Pedro turns back to the cook shack and leans against the doorway. Most of the women have gone now. His mother comes to the doorway and says rather sharply, "Move." He backs slowly out of the way, but stays against the wall watching as she and the sister fill the basket that the sister had brought.

We would predict that, had Pedro been sitting in the doorway in which men were coming in and out, the adult men would have required Pedro to move out of the way and that after one reminder, he would have voluntarily moved away from the door on the approach of any adult male. We would also predict, however, that had a girl of Pedro's age been in the doorway, the women would not have stepped over her but, rather, would have required her to move away if she did not do so without being asked.

From the interview material and the observations, it is fairly clear that mothers, in fact, take more responsibility in the training of daughters than of sons and that fathers take more responsibility for boys. The women that we interviewed frequently made this differentiation explicit. For example, a mother, when asked what she does if her 8-year-old child delays in carrying out a request, replied, "I scold him, but when he does comply, I tell him, 'That's the way to do it; now you're acting like a big boy.'" Then the mother went on to say that the father was stricter than she was. She expressed herself as follows. "That's the way to do it with older children. It hurts me that their father makes them work, that he takes them away from the house when they're so young (speaking of 8- to 10-year-old boys), but I tell myself it's better that way even though it hurts me, because if I leave them alone and don't make them work, if I don't make them do it now, later on, they will turn out to be lazy." She then goes on to express pride in these boys who have just helped their father with the harvesting of the corn crop. In observations, this same mother was seen to allow these boys to get away without following up on requests that she would make to them.

Besides obedience and the learning of new tasks, there are three important new settings in late childhood which require new habits: school, caretaking away from home (e.g., bathing younger siblings in the stream), and work away from home (e.g., gathering wood in the hills or working in the fields with the father). The first new setting affects both sexes, the second is most relevant for girls, and the last primarily involves boys. The important common factor in all of these situations is that they involve being away from the immediate vicinity of the courtyard. Earlier, the child has been accompanied by a parent or an older sibling. Now, for the first time, he may be "on his own" in these new situations. School will be examined first.

Of the three new situations, the school involves the greatest adjustment, since this puts the child into a completely new environment that includes the teacher and students of the central part of town who look down on him and feel that the barrio child is an ignorant, dirty, poor, backward Indian. It is also important to note that it is an environment with which the parents of the present-day barrio children have had no experience, for none of them attended school. We know of only three barrio adults who attended school earlier than 1945. Even now, only about 50% of the barrio children of school age spend a significant amount of time in school. It is true that adult barrio members have learned to interact with the Mexican population of the central town. Most of these interactions, however, are highly patterned, with the barrio Indian definitely taking a subordinate role. Furthermore, most of the interaction between adults of the barrio and the townspeople are at a relatively superficial level and include such things as economic transactions in the market or in the stores of the townspeople. Also, on occasion, townspeople hire barrio persons to do various sorts of menial labor or farm work. The important thing is that the interaction at the adult level lacks the closeness, the constantness, and the intimacy that is inevitable in the school for those barrio children who attend at all regularly.

There are three problems which attending school poses. The barrio child must learn to interact with children who have been reared in very different ways and who react differently from the barrio children; the parents of their new agemates, although preaching equality, treat the barrio people as inferiors; and the language in school is Spanish rather than Mixtecan. And although barrio parents begin to teach their children Spanish around 4 or 5 in anticipation of their going to school, they are still not proficient in the new language. In short, the school involves a radically new and somewhat harsh environment for the barrio child. In discussing the school, we will first describe the general classroom situation and then the relationship between the barrio and central children.

The school is located in the central part of town, about a half a block off from the main square. It is between a mile and a 2-mile walk for the barrio children. By and large, the barrio children do not attend very regularly, with some exceptions to be noted below. The girls' attendance, on the whole, is more regular than that of the boys. Children frequently spend more than one year in the same grade. Of the twenty-four children in our sample, all who were in school were in either the first or the second grade. The school itself is an old, colonial-style house in that the rooms are all in a line and open on an arched corridor about 3 yards wide which faces a large yard. The school itself covers two sides of the yard. This large yard is used for playing.

The first grade teacher is a young woman of about 23 who was born in a neighboring village. She comes from an originally Mixteco family. Although she herself is very definitely of Mexican culture, she has relatives who still identify themselves as Indians. She seems to like her teaching, and she expresses herself in interviews about her own lack of understanding of the Indian children. She says that it irritates her very much that the Indian children speak Mixteco in class all of the time. She believes that the barrio children have a very much lower level of concentration than do the town children. She thinks that the parents of the barrio children are responsible for the lack of attention shown by the Indian children in keeping their copy books clean, attending classes regularly, and so on. In spite of her expressed attitudes, the observations in the classroom seem to indicate that she behaves toward the barrio children without prejudice. As nearly as we could tell from the observations, she gives the barrio children equal opportunity. She does give more attention to boys than to girls, whether Indian or non-Indian.

The teaching method she uses consists of what is called in Mexico the global method. This means that she teaches reading and writing by introducing short, complete words which are formed by a small number of different letters that can be combined in different ways to form a great number of words. She writes the word on the blackboard, reads it aloud, and then has the children copy it in their copybooks. She uses very few visual aids. She accounts for this by saying that the school is very poor. The aids that she does use are small cards with pictures with the word naming the object underneath. There are only a few of these cards, and the children seldom handle them. The only other visual aids that she uses are drawings on the blackboard and colored sheets of paper which she hangs on the wall. On these sheets of paper are simple drawings, words, or mathematical operations. For example, $2 + 2 = 4$, and so forth. Four of the barrio children in our sample were in this classroom.

The other children in the sample are in the second grade, which is taught by a man about 40 years old who has some intellectual prestige in the central part of town. He writes long poems for all national holidays and reads them at the school festivals. While observing in his classroom, it seemed that his behavior was oriented primarily toward impressing the observer. He tended to behave in an authoritarian fashion toward the children and, during the time of our presence, used literary forms of speech which he probably did not use on ordinary occasions. While in his room, we frequently saw definite cases of biased behavior toward the barrio children in his class. Examples of such prejudiced behavior will be given below.

The actual flavor of the classroom can be most vividly obtained by excerpts from an observation made in the classroom itself. The following observation was taken in the second grade. It illustrates several points about the school in general and about the second grade teacher in particular. Note the following points in it:

1. The classroom behavior as a whole is very informal and at times almost chaotic. This feature of constant movement and noise and individual conversations and interactions among the students is typical of almost every single observation we took in the schools.

2. It is to be noted that in the following observation, the teacher is giving out parts of a poem for the children to recite. The recitation of poetry is important to the children in this case, since they will recite at the fiesta on September 16th, which is Mexico's Independence Day and equivalent to our Fourth of July celebration. Thus all the children desire to participate in the fiesta. It is characteristic of the second grade male teacher, when giving out rewards of this sort, to give more opportunity to the children from the central part of town than to the Indian children of the barrio. In the observation below, he gives only one poem to any barrio child, and the way in which he ignores Alberto is typical of his behavior toward all barrio children in this kind of situation.

3. Note how Alberto reacts to the behavior of the teacher by displacing his hurt and aggression onto other students, after being rebuffed by the teacher. As the observation begins, the teacher has been reading poetry out loud and allowing the children to choose which poems they want to recite on Independence Day. The students listen until he finishes, at which time all shout at the same time, "Me, me, teacher, give it to me." The children stand up; the teacher makes them all sit down, and they laugh. As the observation begins, Alberto is sitting on a table with his feet on the chair.

Alberto stretches forward, his arms extended on the table and his body leaning toward his bench, doubled slightly at the waist. The teacher begins to read another poem. Alberto looks at the child who is sitting on his left and says to him, smiling, "This one is pretty." The other smiles also and repeats, "This is pretty." Before the teacher finishes, Alberto stands up on his bench, waves his hand, and shouts, "Me, teacher, me." The child who is next to him stands up and cries, "Me, teacher, me." Alberto, the other boy, and several others get up and run toward the teacher, surrounding him and raising their hands so that he might give them a part of the poem. The teacher hands the poetry to one of the central children. Alberto immediately turns around, and the boy who was his bench companion imitates him. As they are walking back to their seats, Alberto shrugs his shoulders, looks at the other, and says, "There are more."

The other boy sits down, Alberto returns to the teacher and stands facing him and says, "Teacher, shall I take this?" (He was referring to a sheet on which the poetry is written.) The teacher does not answer and begins to read another poem. Alberto returns to his place and sits on the table with his feet hanging toward the aisle, hands folded in his lap. He gets down, sits in his chair, stretches, lowers himself to the floor, and remains there listening. When the poem is finished, he runs down the aisle toward the teacher, but before he gets there, a group of children have already surrounded the teacher. In the middle of all this noise, Alberto raises his hand and says, "Me, teacher, you haven't given me a single one; you're not giving me any." The teacher gives the poem to Alberto's bench companion, who returns to sit down with a broad smile on his face and the paper in his hand.

When Alberto sees the other child with the poem, he again runs to the teacher, who is still surrounded by a group of children. Alberto tries to push apart two of them, sticking his head between the shoulders of the two, and looks over the teacher's arm. The teacher hands the last poem to another central child and says, "Now, there are no more."

Alberto, not getting any, goes back to his seat. Seriously, he looks at the other boy and says, "It's all finished." The child laughingly shows him the poem that he has in his hand. Alberto again returns to the teacher and asks him, "Are they all finished? Isn't there anything for me?" The teacher, who is speaking to another boy, does not answer him. Alberto returns to his bench and sits with his head between his hands. He stand up and shouts, "Teacher." When he doesn't get an answer, he sits down again. He looks at his bench companion and says to him, "Don't bother me." His bench companion laughs and stands up and then sits down again. Alberto hits him, givng him a punch in the stomach. The boy stands up. Alberto raises his foot under the table and gives him a kick at the same time. The other boy leaves, running. He stops a few feet away and looks back at Alberto with a smile. Alberto looks at him seriously. The other child moves away, and when he is a few steps farther away, he looks back and says, "You'll see," and then he goes and sits in another place. Alberto remains looking at the front of the room.

None of the observations taken in the first grade female teacher's room show as clear-cut bias toward barrio children. In the second grade, the barrio children have no effective way of relating to the teacher; rather, they have to adopt a subservient attitude toward him, and there are several examples in the observations of the kind of displaced aggression toward their agemates shown by Alberto in the above account. The first grade teacher does not adopt the superior attitude of the second grade teacher, nor does she ignore the barrio children, as he so typically does. The barrio children are much more frequently rewarded for their efforts at learning in the first grade class than they are in the second.

In the context of the school, the barrio child learns to cope with children from the center of town in various ways that differ from any techniques or behavior used earlier in their interaction with other barrio children. These techniques include the following: an increase in overt aggressive acts, such as hitting and kicking, telling falsehoods and lies about what one owns or what one's customs are in order to save face with central children, and accepting subordinate positions in games with children from the central part of town.

Although they receive some unorganized support and informal instruction from older friends and relatives from the barrio, these new types of behavior are learned primarily in games with age peers. For example, in the game, *carry the word*, barrio children receive practice in hitting in a socially sanctioned (sanctioned by the central part of town standards) context. The following observation on Hidelberto, age 8, in the school courtyard during recess, illustrates the game. The observation begins just as the children are leaving their room for the courtyard; the recess bell has just rung.

Hidelberto leaves the room running and stops just outside the door, where another child takes him by the shirt and asks him, "Don't you have any verse to say?" Hidelberto makes a gesture with his hand as if to say, "What can you do?" and then says with a very special accent, "Didn't you see? Man—they didn't give me any!" The other boy looks very serious, as if someone had died (but observer interprets this as a joke) and says, "I'm sorry, brother, I'm sorry." The two children then laugh together.

Hidelberto runs to the courtyard and gets in a line. The teacher goes back into the room, and the children begin to play a game called *carry the word*. (This game may be described as follows: the first boy in the line hits the one behind him and says to him, "Carry the word." This boy then passes the punch, or the blow, onto the following boy in the line. He is supposed to hit the boy in the line following him in the same place that he received the blow. At the same time, he strikes the next boy and repeats the words, "Carry the word." This is continued all down the line. The joke is that each boy that gets punched is supposed to be unaware of the game; and when he receives it, he passes it quickly to the following boy, so as not to break the chain. The boys make a great point in attempting to give the blow to the person next to him in a way that the other boys in the line do not know that it is coming.)

When the boy next to Hidelberto punches him in the arm and says, "Carry the word," Hidelberto, without turning around, punches the boy behind him and says to him softly, "Carry the word." The boy next to him then passes his punch onto the next.

When the line is finished, Hidelberto and several other boys begin the cycle again, saying, "Carry the word," and hitting the following boy in the line. The game soon becomes disorganized in that it breaks out in several parts of the line. In a few minutes, there is terrible confusion, and all are interchanging punches, laughing and shouting, among them Hidelberto, who hits his line companion three times when he should have hit him but once.

The teacher arrives (the second grade male teacher) and stands in front of the line. The children stop playing. Hidelberto leans one foot on the other and laughs while scratching his head. The boy whom he had hit before takes him by the collar and tries to throw him on the ground. Hidelberto shakes himself until the other boy lets him go. He turns around a few times and asks, "What time do you have?" (*Note:* Technically speaking, these boys do not know how to tell time.) No one answers him.

Other games played in the school context include hitting and other kinds of aggressive acts that would generally not be allowed in the barrio. In our earlier discussion of the socialization of aggression, we pointed out the severity of the barrio practices with respect to aggression and the suppression of any overt aggressive acts. In the school setting, the barrio child is thrown into situations which almost demand the use of some overt aggressive acts. Games, such as *carry the word,* are one of the ways in which barrio children learn to behave aggressively in their interaction with others. A barrio child who has been in school for a few months begins to hit and push beyond the context of play when he interacts with children from the central part of town. Since the school presents many frustrating experiences for the barrio child, we would expect that such frustration would be followed by aggressive acts on his part. And indeed, such is the case. However, most of the aggression on the part of barrio children observed in the school context, or in the central part of town, takes place under "safe" conditions or is displaced or masked in some manner. That is, the barrio child is seldom observed "sticking up for his own rights" in a manner equally aggressive to that of the children from the central part of town. Another response to instigation to aggression by the barrio children is to use some subterfuge to head off the necessity of the use of direct aggression. Techniques used here would include telling falsehoods, ignoring or redirecting the aggression, escaping the situation in some way, or accepting a subordinate position.

The barrio child is usually not able to fight or wrestle with comfort. So long as it is a game, or in fun, he participates with apparent ease, but the moment the situation gets serious, he attempts to retreat or tries to deny or ignore the aggressive component of the interaction with children from the central part of town. In the following observation we see an 8-year-old boy, Jubenal, showing some anxiety when a fight threatens to become serious. His response is to attempt to make a joke out of the whole affair. Significantly, he does not become openly angry, as a central child would probably do. As the observation begins, Jubenal is in the corridor adjacent to the playground, playfully punching with two other children. A group of children are looking at the two boys and laughing. Jubenal and the child with whom he is playing at the moment are roaring with laughter while they pull each other over the corridor, sort of wrestling against each other.

Jubenal and the other boy are scuffling with their arms around one another. Each one has his arms crossing the chest to the shoulder of the other. In spite of the fact that they are both showing strength, they are not apparently trying to harm each other. (It is clearly a game at this point.) The two are roaring with laughter. In one of their movements, they fall to the ground intertwined and scuffle around with first one on top and then the other. They go rolling around on the ground until Jubenal remains above the other boy. At this point, Jubenal stops his efforts. (*Note of observer:* It appears that Jubenal is hoping that the other will stop his efforts also.) While Jubenal looks down at the other boy, laughing and breathing heavily, he pulls up his pants which have slipped down, adjusting his belt with both hands. He is fairly red in the face and is breathing rapidly; his clothes are in disorder and his hair messed up. Both boys stand up and then the other boy begins to run. Jubenal lets out a yell, and runs after him. He catches him, and again they scuffle, with Jubenal's arms around the waist of the other boy. The two run, gripped in this fashion, while all the children who have been watching run behind them, following by a few yards.

Another boy who was following catches up to them and joins in the fray. The three run together through the little passage way in the corridor. Jubenal lets go of the boy and leaves the other two scuffling and fighting, still playfully, and watches them. Another boy comes running from the courtyard and grabs Jubenal from behind, as if he wanted to join in the fight also. Jubenal shakes himself loose, and with a push almost throws the other boy to the ground. Then Jubenal laughs. The two again put their arms on each other's shoulders, fighting and pushing. They both then try, with their arms on the other's shoulders, to entwine the legs of the other so they will fall to the ground. The two boys double at the waist backward and forward, breathing heavily, uttering small groans and ughs. Jubenal grabs the other boy by the shirt and pulls at it as if he wanted to take it off. While he does this, the other boy grabs him by the calf of the leg and throws him to the ground. Jubenal gets up (the other boy stands laughing in an expectant attitude). Again they scuffle, and this time Jubenal throws the other boy to the ground by the same system of grabbing at the legs. The other boy hits the ground quite hard. He gets up, no longer laughing, and grabs Jubenal by the arm, twisting it. Jubenal is laughing; but when he tries to free himself, he becomes rather serious (he just realizes that the other is no longer "playing"—that the other boy has become angry). The other boy then throws Jubenal to the ground. From the ground, where Jubenal is sitting, he says to the boy, "What are you doing?" The other boy raises him from the ground by pulling him by the arm and begins to shake him. Jubenal laughs again. The other child lets him go and runs through the courtyard. Jubenal adjusts his trousers and begins to run after him, following him with shouts. The children run round and round, taking turns chasing each other; they climb some stairs, they come back down, they run between other children pushing them and return, running through the corridor where they were. There they begin to fight again by interlocking their arms and placing their hands on the other's shoulders. The other child throws Jubenal to the ground between laughs. Jubenal falls on his back, and as the other let him go suddenly, his head hits the ground rather hard. With tears in his eyes, Jubenal cries and laughs at the same time, with the other children who are watching also laughing.

(Finally, Jubenal conquers the cry part and again laughs with the other children and begins playing again in a much more subdued manner.)

A child from the central part of town would have reacted to the last hard blow with anger and would not have shown as much self-control, nor would he have tried to fit into the group by making a joke and ignoring, insofar as possible, his apparently painful blow on the head. The observàtions in the barrio showed only scattered examples of boys scuffling with each other, and in none of our observations did they end in fights. In contrast, our informal observations in the school play yard indicated that scuffles ending in fights among children from the central part of town were not at all unusual. Barrio boys, in this school situation, avoided bringing such an episode to a close with overt aggression. By the time they reach the second grade, some of the barrio children begin to approach the direct expression of aggression, and on occasion, they use verbal aggression but generally avoid physical aggression. The following observation illustrates three aspects of aggressive behavior, or responses to aggressive behavior, on the part of a barrio boy. One is the use of verbal aggression against a central boy in defense of a friend from the barrio; the second is response to an aggressive act by the teacher; and the third is the response of ignoring aggression by a boy from the central part of town. This observation involves Jubenal again, who is sitting next to another boy from the barrio, Hidelberto. As the observation begins, Jubenal and Hidelberto are sitting together on the same bench at a table.

Jubenal is sitting, looking straight ahead, slapping the palms of his hands on the top of the table. (He appears relaxed and contented.) A boy from the central part of town walks down the aisle and makes a hitting gesture at Hidelberto, who is sitting next to Jubenal. Immediately Jubenal stands up on the bench and says, "This son of a gun," and pretends he is going to climb down and chase after the other child, who has by this time gotten out of the way. The teacher sees him and cries out, "What are you doing—one moment," and takes a few steps toward Jubenal with a little rod in his hand. (This rod is frequently carried by this male second grade teacher. During our observations, he frequently threatened with it, although he never actually struck a child in the presence of the observer. The children reported that he hits them with this rod on occasion.) Jubenal reacts immediately, sitting himself down on the bench, in a restful position but very straight, hands together quietly on the table, feet crossed one over the other. The teacher returns to his former position and turns his back.

When the teacher is not looking, Jubenal, from across the room, makes signs at the child who had made the hitting gesture at Hidelberto, as if indicating with his fist that he's going to get even later. (The gesture that he uses is a conventional one, and in Mexico is a defiant gesture that implies, "I'll take care of you later.")

Jubenal turns forward in his seat and speaks a few words to the boy in front of him in Mixteco. The teacher slaps the rod on the blackboard, asking the class to be quiet again. Jubenal sits up straighter than ever, seriously looking at a little girl who is standing in front of the class and who now begins to recite. He listens with much interest, hands joined, eyes fixed on the little girl, without moving himself for a few moments. (He was sitting almost rigid.) When the little girl finishes reciting, a central boy comes and punches him quite strongly in the back. Jubenal turns around and looking over his shoulder, he smiles at the boy who struck him. At this moment, another girl begins to recite, and Jubenal returns to his previous attitude, listening with much interest.

In this observation, the verbal and gestural aggression in the early part toward a central boy was a "safe" type of behavior for Jubenal in that there was the protection of the school class situation, and it was of a minor enough sort that it would not be followed up. The use of a threatening gesture with the rod by the teacher was immediately responded to, and in our observations was always responded to, by the students, although it is to be noted that immediately upon the teacher's turning his back, the students went right back to their horseplay. Jubenal's response of smiling at the boy who hit him rather hard in the back was quite clearly a refusal to return in kind the aggression of the boy from the center of town.

An example of telling a falsehood in response to what was probably a derogatory question from a child from the central part of town is contained in the following excerpt from an observation. This observation was taken in the first grade in the presence of the female teacher. Angel, the subject of this episode, was sitting in one of the front benches surrounded by a group of children, some standing, some sitting, some writing, and some chatting. The teacher is standing next to the group, talking with some of the children. Every once in a while she walks up and down the aisles looking at the rest of the children.

As the teacher moves away, Angel turns and follows her with his eyes. The teacher says, "Write 'as.' " Angel looks at his notebook, laughs, and writes, copying the notebook of the child seated to his left. He raises the notebook and shows it to the teacher, saying, "Is there an 'a' missing?" The teacher looks at it and says, "Yes, the 'a.' " Angel writes in the notebook and then puts down his pencil. Then he picks his notebook up in both hands, putting it on top of his head. The child who is seated in the seat ahead of him and who is from the central part of town turns around and asks him, "In your house, do you have a well?" "Yes," answers Angel. (This is not true.) Angel looks at him and says, "Look, look here," and passes his book rapidly before the other's eyes. "Fine," answers the other boy.

Angel gets up, stands on the chair, leans his hands on the table, and looks at what the child on the bench in front is writing. He wrinkles his forehead. He sits down again, stretches out, turns his notbook over, stands up and puts his elbow on the table, sucking the pencil in his mouth. The teacher looks at his notebook and says, "Let's see." Angel shows it to her. The teacher says, "Yes, now you've got it." She smiles at him. Angel looks at his benchmate, but this child is looking the other way. The teacher says, "Now, you're going to write the word 'chair.'" Angel writes rapidly in his notebook and raises it immediately, showing it, and saying, "Like this?" The teacher glances at him rapidly, saying, "No, not like that. There is a letter missing." Angel puts the notebook down and writes again. He raises it and repeats, "Like this?" "Yes, very good," says the teacher approvingly. Angel throws the notebook in the air and cries out, "Ay, ay, ay!" laughing contentedly and showing his notebook to the child next to him.

Another child from the center of town gets up and comes toward the teacher, standing between the teacher and Angel. He says to Angel, "Let's see the pencil." Angel withdraws the hand in which he has the pencil and does not give it to the boy. "Let's see," says the other, and he grabs the pencil from Angel's hand with a jerk. Angel smiles, and he gently removes the pencil again from the boy's hand. Then Angel holds the pencil tightly in his fist, pounding it on the table, and at the same time, tapping the ground with his foot. He closes the notebook and continues pounding on the table as he looks out at the street through the open door of the room.

There are three typical and characteristic actions to note in this observation. First is the use of a falsehood to head off a possible derogatory sequence, such as when the child from the center of town asks about a well. Angel responded to this question with a quick lie and then distracted the boy's attention with an irrelevant comment and gesture with his notebook. The second item of special note is the difference between the female teacher of some Mixteco background toward barrio children and the male second grade teacher who discriminates against the barrio children and never gives them a warm response. Angel's increased efforts and interest followed dramatically from her warm and reinforcing remarks and smiles. A third item of note in the observation was Angel's response to the boy who jerked his pencil from his hand. Angel's response of a smile to this somewhat aggressive act and his subsequent gentle removal of the pencil from the boy's hand typifies the subordinate position which the barrio children frequently assumed, and it shows how a smile may be used in an attempt to head off further aggressive acts on the part of town children. We have seen that attendance at school by barrio children requires many adjustments on their part. It is clear that previous behavior patterns are not sufficient to cope with the school situation and that behaviors and techniques rarely used in the barrio occur with great frequency in the school setting. In addition to the setting of the school itself, we should also mention an additional factor, that in order to get to school, the children are required to go through several blocks in the central area of town.

This brings them into contact with the central children who are playing in the streets and who frequently have some kind of interaction with the barrio children as they pass by. As younger children, any experiences a barrio child may have in the center of town are always buffered by the presence of an older caretaker. Even these experiences would generally be confined to small economic exchanges of a sort that do not entail extended and informal interpersonal relations with town children. Barrio children are discriminated against by the town children. In fact, many of the barrio parents report that the reason their children do not attend school is because the central children are aggressive toward them or hit them on their way to school. The parents will keep the barrio children at home rather than subject them to the aggressions of the town children. The following observation characterizes the relationship in the street between the children in the central part of town and the barrio children. In this observation, Jubenal is walking through the street returning from school. He is walking with another barrio child who is carrying a wooden hoe. Jubenal is carrying his own school books under his arm.

The two boys walk alongside one another in silence. In the middle of the street ahead of them, there are some central children playing a form of baseball. As they approach the group, Jubenal and the other child stop to look. Jubenal smiles at the children and makes motions as if he were going after the ball. (Quite obviously he wants them to invite him to play. The central children would probably not make such motions without being invited.) The boy with whom Jubenal was walking continues to walk while Jubenal stops. Jubenal watches him moving away, but he himself does not move. Jubenal begins to shout, "Now play. . . ." (It appeared as if his presence was being noted, but he breaks off his encouragement or statement in the middle.) The other child who was walking with Jubenal is now beyond the group and quite a distance from Jubenal. Jubenal looks at him and goes on walking very slowly and walking backward, still watching the game. The other boy stops, and when Jubenal catches up with him, he says to him, "Shall we play?" The other boy stands leaning on his hoe. Jubenal continues looking at the players and smiling. The other children from the center of town continue playing, but they do not recognize his presence nor do they invite him to join them. Jubenal remains serious, looking at the children with one hand in his mouth. When one of the children passes close to him, he smiles at him, but the central child does not pay any attention to him.

Jubenal, looking serious, scrapes his teeth with a finger. When another central child comes close to him, Jubenal cries out to him encouragingly, "How you play, eh?" The central child ignores him as if he didn't see him. Jubenal seems more serious. He puts his hands in his pockets and continues looking. The other barrio child puts his hoe on his shoulder and touches Jubenal's shoulder without talking, gesturing that they leave. Jubenal turns around, and the two go down the street, walking slowly. They pass by a small girl from the center of town. When they get next to her, Jubenal gives her a little kick which just misses her, and she shies away. When they get a few yards ahead of the girl, she takes a stone and throws it at Jubenal. It doesn't hit him, but the boys hear the noise and turn around and look at her. When they are about 25 yards from the baseball players, Jubenal turns around once more and looks at them; then he continues walking alongside his companion.

In addition to providing a vivid description of the general tenor of everyday interaction between the central and barrio children, the above observation again contains an example of displaced aggression, this time toward the little girl from town.

In our discussion of late childhood up to this point, our evidence has been based primarily on observational material and on the mother interviews. In reviewing the state of the various behavior systems in late childhood, we also have the evidence from the TAT questions administered to the children in this period. In the following discussion, we will review the evidence obtained from the TAT and child interview questions and attempt to interpret the answers in terms of the various behavior systems; then we will relate this interpretation to the evidence already presented. It is clear that the children's responses to the TAT questions represent a different level of data from that of the observation protocols and the remarks of the mothers in the interview situation. However, by combining evidence from each of these three sources, we should reach a better understanding of the behavior systems of late childhood.

The child's attitude concerning aggression is well illustrated in the responses to the TAT questions and the story situations for children. In general, the child will not admit to open aggression, even in his verbal responses to the story situations. For example, in response to the question, "A child is sitting under a tree. Another child passes, trips on a branch and falls, then he stops and says to the seated child, 'Why did you trip me?' But the seated child didn't do anything. What happens?" In only one response was there any resulting aggression shown in the story given in response to this situation. In the vast majority of cases, the child attributed blame to the other, but then went home and told his mother. In response to the direct question, "If another child hits you, what do you do?" the typical answer for both sexes would be represented by the following response. "I cry. No, I do not hit him, I tell his mother so that she will scold him." The aggression here is rather veiled in that one may tattle on another but would not engage in any overt aggression even though it was initiated by another person. This verbal response on the part of the children in answer to a hypothetical situation of direct instigation to aggression corresponds quite closely to the observations in the school, where the child, in fact, meets many occasions where other children instigate aggression. The denial of direct physical counter-attack in the TAT and interview responses corresponds to the infrequent use of direct counterattack to aggressive acts in the school situation. The counterpart to the veiled aggression implied in tattling in the TAT responses comes out in the observation protocols in the form of displaced aggression against a relatively harmless person or object and in "safe" types of verbal or gestural aggression.

Although there was only one example of direct aggression in the first person, the barrio children were able to tell aggressive stories if they did not involve the idea of any overt aggression on the part of the child himself. For example, stories told about the following situation frequently contained aggressive answers. "A child is standing in the middle of the street. An angry bull comes running down the street. What happens?" This situation is rather common in the barrio environment, and about 50% of the children indicated that the child went into a doorway, or that someone helped him into a doorway, or some functional equivalent of this response. On the other hand, approximately 50% of the responses indicated that the child was injured by the bull, and in 2 cases out of 12, that the child was killed by the bull. In the cases in which the child was injured by the bull, there was an immediate attempt on the part of some actor in the story, generally a mother or elder sister, to fix or mend or comfort the injured child. Thus 50% of the children were able to report and verbalize an aggressive act on the part of an animal, in this case, in a situation which does not involve them personally in direct physical aggression. In the observational protocols, we have several examples presented above where barrio children were able to engage in games, such as *carry the word,* that involved hitting and direct physical aggressive techniques in the guise of a play situation. This may be somewhat equivalent to shifting blame or, at the least, shifting responsibility for aggressive acts from oneself, that is, when aggressive techniques are used under the guise of play, the child does not see himself responsible for the use of direct aggression.

Two of the behavior systems, namely achievement and self-reliance, are very difficult to distinguish from each other as they operate in barrio children. With respect, for example, to a question such as, "If you're doing something and it's very difficult, what do you do?" more than half of the children of both sexes indicated that they would simply leave the situation; only one child's response indicated any value or emphasis placed on attempting to try harder or to persevere and keep at the task. Now, whether the fact that a difficult task would be abandoned indicates a lack of achievement orientation or a lack of self-reliance is a fine point. On the whole, we would tend to interpret it as involving both behavior systems. Neither are developed to any great extent in the typical barrio child.

In only 1 of the 24 mother interviews was there any emphasis placed on achievement. In the other 23 cases, there were no indications that the mother desired her child to strive to do things better than other children. The whole conception seems to be a desire that each child will learn to perform up to some minimum standard, but that there is no value in nor desire to go beyond this. It is generally taken for granted that all individuals will easily learn to perform up to these standards. For example, with respect to the task of learning to make tortillas, every mother would expect her daughter to make acceptable tortillas, but there would be no emphasis on making better tortillas than other women. In fact, the question simply would never arise. The situation is the same with respect to all of the normal skills and tasks generally engaged in by people in the barrio.

One variant case is of great interest in that it stands out in great contrast from the other families in the sample. This concerns a family in which the mother came from outside the barrio and from a Mexican family, so that marriage into the barrio was a definite lowering of status from her point of view. She is married to the only adult male in the barrio who does not support himself primarily by raising corn and beans. He works in the central part of town as a secretary in the mayor's office. He is one of the three adult males in the barrio who are considered literate. The mother dresses more like the people in the central part of town than like the women in the barrio. In addition, the husband's drinking patterns were more nearly like those in the center part of town. Also, he did not participate in the ceremonies of the barrio but rather was attempting to identify himself with the townspeople. He was the only person in the barrio that we observed who became aggressive when he drank. Thus, on several points, they were a variant family. By examining this mother's responses on the mother interview, we can illustrate the patterns of the other 23 mothers in comparison. This mother, in response to the question, "What work or task is expected of your child daily or weekly?" had the following to say:

He takes care of his burros, goes on errands for me, keeps the weeds down. He has himself four donkeys. He wasn't crazy. His uncle had an old female donkey which he was going to kill because she was ill and was no good any more for carrying things. The uncle said to my boy, "Do you want that burro?" He didn't think that the boy would say anything, but the boy said, "Yes, I do." After a short while, the donkey had a little son and then a little daughter and now, there are four of them altogether, and my boy takes care of them. He says, "You see, Mother, now I have 400 pesos all for myself. Some day I'll be able to sell my burros, and then after that, I'll get some more." Well, I think the boy is not so dumb to do that, and I tell him, "Very good, my son. You're doing very well. Guard your money. Don't turn out to be poor like your father." My husband certainly doesn't mistreat me, nor did he turn into a drunk, but he's pretty fouled up (i.e., poor). It's hard, you know, for me because my father had a lot of property and money. We even used to have cheese balls to sell, but when I left my house to get married, I became so poor and that's why it's better for my boy to be bright and take good care of his donkeys. He doesn't load wood; he only takes care of his donkeys now and does a few little things for me. When he's bigger, at about 16 or 17, he'll learn to work the ox team in the field. That's the only work there is here for men; but before that, he'll have to go to school. I don't want him to turn out to be as stupid as those of the barrio because—yes, we are very stupid, as I, for example, don't know what you are writing down on the paper, and it hurts me. Yes, he'll go to school.

This is the only example out of 23 responses to the question that contains any hint of an emphasis on achievement. The other mothers simply listed a few tasks and ended up by saying something like, "That's all." None of the other mothers volunteered any comments that would indicate that there was any awareness of a desire for the children to achieve above others. There were two mothers who mentioned casually, as a fact, that their children were going to school, but they did not indicate that this was in order to better themselves.

With respect to self-reliance, it seems that most mothers take self-reliant behavior on the part of their children for granted; there was no indication that they consciously encouraged self-reliance, although there are examples in the behavioral observation that can be interpreted as a parent allowing a child to attempt tasks that he could just barely handle when it would have been easier for the parent to step in and help. These cases probably represent some direct training for self-reliance.

The mother in the variant family, whose remarks were quoted above to illustrate her unique emphasis on achievement, differs in a systematic way from the other mothers in behavior systems other than achievement and self-reliance. For example, she is somewhat more defensive than the barrio women in general. It is our hypothesis that the severity and effectiveness of training with respect to suppressing overt aggression in the barrio children is inherently incompatible with the development of strong achievement drives and emphasis on the development of self-reliance. We would assume that a strong achievement orientation would necessarily involve competition, and that if the fear of expressing aggression is strong enough, effective competition would not be allowed to develop. If this is true, it follows that individuals who place high emphasis on achievement must, or would probably, handle aggression training differently than those who do not place emphasis on achievement.

It is interesting to look at the variant mother who expressed strong desires for achievement on the part of her son and to see how she handles the training of aggression for him. If our hypothesis is correct, we would expect her to be variant on the handling of aggression as a consequence, or at least, as related to her emphasis on achievement. As mentioned earlier, we asked all the mothers, "What do you wish (name of child) to do if another child looks for an argument with him, or when another child wishes to fight with him?" Every single mother in the sample, except this variant mother, indicated that she would not want her child to fight. In addition, every single mother, except the case in point, indicated that she would apply disciplinary action for fighting in the situation. The mother who encourages achievement and self-reliance gave the following answer, which is in distinct contrast to the other 23 mothers.

I tell him not to look for an argument, but if someone else does, I tell him to stand up and fight. I tell him to only fight with his hands. He should not pick up a stone or anything, because that way you can hurt people. I tell him it's shameful. I tell him don't be rude, but don't give in either, because it's bad to have people get used to that.

This one case suggests, although the data do not allow validation, that low achievement and self-reliance are related to the extreme fear of aggressive behavior shown in the sample as a whole. Strong achievement strivings would seem to require the willingness to express some aggressive impulses. We do not wish to suggest any direct causal relationship but only to indicate that the three variables are interrelated in the training of barrio children.

The TAT questions revealed some interesting attitudes on the part of the children with respect to the behavior systems of nurturance and sociability. It is at the beginning of late childhood that the child is no longer nurtured for small accidents or difficulties into which he gets himself. This is one of the more trying things for a child, the fact that he is no longer comforted on occasions that would have elicited nurturant and comforting responses on the part of his mother when he was younger. In answer to the question on the TAT item, "What happens when many children are playing in the street and one is alone, standing nearby just watching?" a certain ambivalence with respect to showing nurturant sociability behavior revealed itself. There was also a sex differentiation apparent here. For the girls, two thirds of them gave an answer that indicated in the first part of the answer that the child would be ignored and left standing, and then later in the answer, the child would be invited to join the group. The following answer is typical of this two-thirds. "He just watches them. He is sad because he can't play too. No, they don't call him, but I tell him, 'Come, little child, come play with us,' or 'Come, let us play.' " There were four almost identical answers to this question, and it indicates a certain ambivalence in that the child is first left standing and then given nurturance and invited to join the group. The other third of the girls who responded to this question revealed no ambivalence, and their first and only response was one of inviting the other child to play, which indicated a straightforward nurturant and sociable response. For the boys, two thirds responded that they would just leave him there, and he would feel sad. Typical response of the boys would be, "Nothing. They don't say anything to him. He's just standing there." The other third of the boys would invite the child to play with them. A typical response of this sort is, "I start playing with him because the others don't call him, because they are playing a lot, and he has come all alone."

In balance, the girls responded with more nurturant and sociable responses than the boys in that all girls indicated that they would eventually make a nurturant or sociable response, even though two thirds of them would first let the child stand there without making an immediate response. On the other hand, only a third of the boys made any nurturant or sociable response. Another interesting thing in these replies from the children is that in every case where nurturance is given, it is phrased in the first person, with an implication that the other people do not invite him to play and that they are leaving him out. This, in a sense, would seem to be another example that indicates a shifting of blame or responsibility to others. This shifting of blame is associated with another idea mentioned earlier, namely, that tattling to one's mother is a common and typical response. For example, in answer to the question, "If another child hits you, what do you do?", the majority of both sexes indicated that they would tell their mothers.

The difference between the responses of boys and girls on the TAT items relating to nurturance and sociability as reported above relates to the differences in roles in late childhood. This difference in roles between boys and girls is further emphasized in a definite bifurcation of two new settings for the child of this age. These settings are caretaking away from home, for example, taking a younger sibling up to the river for a bath, and work in the fields for boys. Caretaking of younger siblings in settings in which the mother is not present inherently requires many nurturant responses on the part of a child toward a younger sibling under her care. That a caretaker sometimes delays a nurturant response toward a younger sibling, or sometimes gives a nurturant response only begrudgingly, is reflected in the TAT protocols reported above by the ambivalence of the answer given by the majority of the girls. There is ample documentation in the observational protocols that caretakers of this age frequently postpone or give nurturant responses in a begrudging manner. The fact that the boys begin going to the fields at this age and are not normally pressed into service as caretakers would allow them to offer or refuse to make a nurturant response with no particular ambivalence, and this is reflected in their responses; as we saw, two thirds of them chose not to make a nurturant response in the TAT situation. This also foreshadows the adult differentiation of nurturance, where the mother, in general, gives many more nurturant responses to her children than does the father.

Just as nurturance would seem to be an important behavior system with respect to the caretaking role, so we might expect that the boys' work in the fields would be connected with the behavior system of self-reliance. The observational protocols, however, do not seem to differentiate the sexes in any clear manner with respect to self-reliance. Actions on the part of the children that can be interpreted as self-reliant occur in the observations of both boys and girls. This may well relate to the fact that the caretaking role requires as many actions that we would interpret as self-reliant as does working in the fields. In any event, even though acts occur in the observation that we would interpret as self-reliant, we can find little, if any, explicit emphasis on it in the mother interviews and in the responses to the story situation.

BIBLIOGRAPHY

Beals, Ralph. Ethnology of the Western Mixe. *University of California Publications in American Archaeology and Ethnology*, 1945, 42, 1.

Dahlgren de Jordan, Barbro. *La Mixteca: Su Cultura e Historia Prehispanica*. Mexico: Imprinta Universitaria, 1954.

Fuente, Julio de la. *Yalalag, Una Villa Zapoteca Serrana*. Mexico: Museo Nacional de Antropologia, 1949.

Gay, Jose A. *Historia de Oaxaca*. Departamento de Educación del Gobierno del Estado, Oaxaca, Mexico, 1933.

Lewis, Oscar. *Life in a Mexican Village: Tepoztlán Restudied*. Urbana, Ill.: University of Illinois Press, 1951.

Parsons, Elsie Clews. *Mitla, Town of Souls.* Chicago: University of Chicago Press, 1936.

Pena, M. T. de la. Problemas sociales e económicos de las Mixtecas. *Memorias del Instituto Nacional Indigenista,* 1950, **2,** 1.

Redfield, Robert. *Tepoztlán: A Mexican Village.* Chicago: University of Chicago Press, 1930.

Whetten, Nathan L. *Rural Mexico.* Chicago: University of Chicago Press, 1948.

Index